The Historical Series of the Refo  in America

No. 1

ECUMENISM AND THE REFORMED CHURCH

by

HERMAN HARMELINK III

WM. B. EERDMANS PUBLISHING CO.
GRAND RAPIDS, MICHIGAN

Herman Harmelink III

Printed in the United States of America

For
Barbara and Alan

The Historical Series of the Reformed Church in America

This series has been inaugurated by the General Synod of the Reformed Church in America acting through its Commission on History for the purpose of encouraging historical research and providing a medium wherein this knowledge may be shared both with the academic community and with the members of the denomination in order that a knowledge of the past may contribute to right action in the present.

General Editors

The Rev. Donald J. Bruggink, Ph.D., Western Theological Seminary

The Rev. Elton J. Bruins, Ph.D., Hope College

The Rev. James Z. Nettinga, Th.D., The American Bible Society

Contents

Editor's Preface

The historian will immediately recognize this volume as a valuable contribution to the history of the Reformed Church in America, dealing as it does with the question of its ecumenical relations from 1628 to the present. This benefit to the entire Church has been noted by Robert T. Handy in his Foreword, and need not be repeated here.

But the fact that this particular volume was chosen to begin this historical series in a year when the church is struggling with the question of the specific ecumenical action of organic union with the Presbyterian Church in the United States will undoubtedly raise some questions as to the propriety of the Commission's choice. The author, Herman Harmelink III, is chairman of General Synod's Committee of Interchurch Relations and a well known advocate of church union. His involvement in the ecumenical endeavor is underlined by the fact that his reading of page proofs for this volume was done while an advisor to the World Council of Churches' General Assembly at Uppsala.

The question of propriety can be answered only by dealing with the more fundamental question of the purpose of historical writing. In short, what good is history? Is history of merely antiquarian interest for people who would prefer true stories to novels? If so, then it might be considered in poor taste to tell this story at this time. The Commission has, however, felt it propitious to publish this particular volume now because history has value as a means to understanding. In this specific instance, history has value as a means to understanding our past in reference to the whole spectrum of ecumenical relations. For example, this volume makes it apparent that the impetus for union is not some new thing imposed from above by the denominational bureaucracy, but an integral part of the life of the church which has been at work in various forms throughout its history. It should also be apparent why the Midwest receives each proposal for union with such concern. And, should the present union with the Presbyterian Church in the

United States fail, this volume will be doubly valuable in showing the true nature of the hesitancy of the church in order that the underlying difficulties may be resolved before the denomination is racked by another proposal for union. This history is offered with the hope that as people grow in an awareness of the interplay of events that have shaped their past, they may be more able to understand the interplay of events in which they must make their own decisions.

Fortunately, in recent decades historians have no longer felt it necessary to claim objectivity toward their subject matter. Mr. Harmelink is a proponent of ecumenism and need make no effort to disguise the fact. The real test of the historian, however, is whether or not he has treated his material with fairness. Is the past as he has represented it? Has he quoted both sides honestly? Has he represented all positions adequately? Obviously, the editors and the Commission feel that this volume satisfactorily meets these tests. This should not, however, be interpreted to mean that they agree with all of the positions of the author.

Ecumenism and the Reformed Church is published by the Commission as a reliable history of the ecumenical stance of the Reformed Church in America. It has been provided with thorough documentation in order that those who would investigate further, whether in agreement or disagreement, may have every assistance in so doing. It is the purpose of this historical series not to impose opinions, but to furnish both data and hypotheses which each of us may combine with our own experience in order to come to our own conclusions. For our decisions must not be made on the basis of emotion, or the appearances of the moment, but with a thorough knowledge of what has taken place in the past, that it may form one part of our store of understanding with which we seek to guide the present toward the future.

Donald J. Bruggink
Western Theological Seminary
Holland, Michigan

Foreword

In the 1960's the burgeoning ecumenical movement, once largely a preserve of the experts, attracted wide public attention. The deepening of the ecumenical concern of the Roman Catholic Church, made clear through the Second Vatican Council (1962-65), the launching of many dialogues with other communions, and the greatly increased cooperation in movements for the common good, has received wide and favorable comment. The continued growth of the World Council of Churches, symbolized in its assemblies at New Delhi (1961) and Uppsala (1968), and the participation of world, national, state and local councils of churches in certain types of social concern and action, has provoked considerable discussion. In the United States, the organization of the Consultation on Church Union in 1962, its increase from four to nine participating denominations, and its steady movement toward the preparation of specific plans for the merger of a number of communions, has dramatized another aspect of ecumenical endeavor—the actual union of churches.

These ecumenical developments have deepened interest in the history of church cooperation and unitive effort, and have led historians to look afresh at their materials and interpretations from an ecumenical perspective. This book is an illuminating example of this approach. The author, the Rev. Herman Harmelink III, turns his attention to the ecumenical history of his own communion, The Reformed Church in America, with particular emphasis on the quest for organic union. He tells his story against the background of the clear unitive goals of the Reformed tradition, and with a steady awareness of the general history of the Dutch Reformed people in America, a history which discloses a genuine commitment to cooperation in mission. There has also been a sustained interest in church union among the Dutch Reformed; in the 1890's union with the Reformed Church in the United States [German Reformed] was favored by nine-tenths of the churches and over two-thirds of the Classes—but it did not happen. Harmelink explains how the differences between eastern and western branches of his church, differences stemming largely from the variations between earlier and later streams of immigration from the Netherlands, have so far

3

prevented the consummation of this or a number of other proposed unions. This is a fascinating story of ecumenical action and reaction, of unitive thrust and parry. The work casts light on why the Reformed Church has recently entered discussions with the Presbyterian Church in the United States [Southern Presbyterian] with a view to possible union, and why it has voted not to become a participating member of the Consultation on Church Union.

This case study, however, is of use not only to those interested in the Reformed tradition, but to anyone interested in church union. For many churches have problems somewhat analogous to the ones studied here—many American denominations have branches shaped in part out of variant streams of immigration, and most communions have pro- and anti-union parties in them. Not a few bodies have moved toward union—some with those of their own denominational family, others with those of another confessional heritage—and have then retreated. This monograph, by tracing one church's experiences in detail, can help others to see their own situation in a clearer light. Hopefully, this study will encourage other historians to undertake similar researches. Especially helpful would be an examination of a denomination that did follow its ecumenical drive into union. The German Reformed Church, for example, merged with the Evangelical Synod (1934) and then with the Congregational Christian Churches to form the United Church of Christ (1957). A careful study of this process together with an examination of the present situation of people and congregations once German Reformed would provide a helpful complementary study to the one at hand.

Mr. Harmelink has clearly demonstrated his qualifications for undertaking the research and interpretation that makes this book so useful. A graduate of Central College (B.A., 1954) and Columbia University (M.A., 1955), he received a B.D. from New Brunswick Theological Seminary (1958) and an S.T.M. from Union Theological Seminary (1964). He has studied also at Heidelberg and London and is continuing study toward the doctorate at Union. A pastor of the Reformed Church in Woodcliff-on-Hudson, New Jersey, he is chairman of the Committee on Interchurch Relations of his communion.

It is fairly clear that Christian churches must undergo some fairly sweeping changes in this last third of the twentieth century if they are to fulfill their mission in a troubled time. There is no virtue in change for the sake of change—it is the nature and direction of the changes which are so important. This book provides some historical perspectives which can inform the important work of ecumenical thought and action today and tomorrow.

Robert T. Handy
Professor of Church History
Union Theological Seminary, New York

I
Introduction

The Reformed Church in America, a member of the sisterhood of Reformed and Presbyterian churches around the world and standing in the Calvinistic tradition, should by heritage, theology, and inclination be an ecumenical church. John Calvin never thought of the Reformation as a destruction of the catholicity of the Christian church. He was prepared to cross ten oceans to further the unity of Protestantism, and the numerous letters he wrote to various Protestant leaders throughout Europe testify to his strong ecumenical urge. Nijenhuis calls him "Calvinus Oecumenicus."[1]

The first Dutch Reformed Church in the world was born in an ecumenical setting. Under the rule in the Netherlands of Charles V and his son, Philip II, early converts to Calvinism were not free to practise their religion there and fled abroad, many of them going to England. In London they were welcomed by King Edward VI, head of the newly-independent Church of England, who gave them as their sanctuary the monastery of the Augustinian Friars, which order had been disestablished by Edward's father, Henry VIII. Jan a Lasco, the Polish baron who led the Dutch Reformed Church of Austin Friars in its first years and wrote its liturgy which forms the basis of the present-day liturgy of the Reformed Church in America, was a close friend of Archbishop Cranmer and collaborated with him on many projects.[2]

The creedal statements of the Reformed Church also had ecumenical origins and connections. In addition to the three catholic creeds which are common to most of Christendom, The Apostles' Creed, the Nicene Creed, and the Athanasian Creed, the Reformed Church also recognizes the Heidelberg Catechism, the Belgic Confession, and the Canons of the Synod of Dort. The Belgic Confession (1561), the oldest of these, was not widely received, being accepted only by the Dutch Reformed Churches. The second, the Heidelberg Catechism (1563), was written by Zachary Baer (Ursinus) and Caspar Olevianus, in an attempt to draw together the Lutheran and Reformed elements in the Palatinate. It has been described as having "Lutheran inwardness, Melanchthonian clearness, Zwinglian simplicity, and Calvinistic fire, harmoniously blended."[3] It was accepted only by the Reformed and Presbyterian churches, but widely so: in Germany, Hungary, the Netherlands, Poland, Transylvania, and the United States; and is thus a common bond for the world Reformed family. The Canons of the Synod of Dort, prepared by the international and "ecumenical" Synod held in 1618-19, were signed not only by the Dutch delegates, but by the official delegates of the (Anglican) Church of England (bishops among them), as well as those from churches in the Palatinate, Hesse, Switzerland, Geneva, Bremen, Emden, and France.[4]

With such an ecumenical background, one might expect the Reformed Church in America to have a strong ecumenical inclination, at least toward sister Reformed and Presbyterian churches if not toward other Protestant churches. And indeed she has, but with one very definite reservation: a refusal (thus far) to enter into organic union with any other denomination. Although all her overseas mission activity has been carried out in union with other denominations, and although she has, in this country, consistently allied herself with other denominations in cooperative ventures and councils, she has for over 300 years of history in America maintained her own independent existence. It will be the purpose of the present work to explore the reasons for this contradiction in the life of the Reformed Church, by which she has exhibited genuine interest in and concern for Christian unity but great hesitancy about church union.

The reasons may be found largely in non-theological factors, chief of which are:

a) Dutch provincialism and conservatism and

b) The secessionist history and spirit of the Western (19th-century Dutch) branch of the church.

To be sure, the Eastern (17th-century Dutch) branch of the Reformed Church was historically very conservative, with a concern for adherence to the Doctrinal Standards, but even stronger was her devotion to her Dutch heritage. The Dutch Reformed Church was her means of maintaining ethnic unity and distinctiveness. But as the concern for ethnic distinctiveness began to break down in the Eastern branch of the church, and she was coming into a broader understanding of Christianity and ecumenicity (the latter third of the nineteenth century), she received into her membership a stream of Dutch immigrants whose background was that of the 19th-century Dutch secessions. The Eastern branch's desire to unite with sister denominations was stymied by the "come-out" separatism of the Western seceders at the turn of the century.[5] Since that time the Western branch of the church has grown at a more rapid rate than the Eastern branch, until it now has approximately one-half of the total membership. It has also, since the 1920's, developed a biblical and creedal literalism, based on a narrow interpretation of "doctrinal purity," which has made it reluctant to relate itself to others. Because of the Constitutional requirement that at least two-thirds of the Classes approve of any plan for church union before it can be achieved, the Western branch can prevent any union. But because the cooperative work in which the church is engaged, both in councils and in overseas work, cannot be undone except by a majority, the Eastern branch is able to maintain this expression of Christian unity. Thus the old Eastern and newer Western branches of the church live together and work together within the same household in a somewhat uneasy, but also perhaps somewhat healthy, tension.

II
The Struggle For Ecclesiastical Independence
(1628-1771)

The first Dutch Reformed Church in America was founded in 1628 in Manhattan, then part of the Dutch colony of Nieuw Nederland. For the first 36 years of its existence, it held the privileged position of being the Established Church in the colony as it had been in the homeland. The leaders of the colony's political life were also leaders in the church. No other religion was to be allowed except the Reformed,[1] but in fact good relations were maintained by the Reformed with the Roman Catholics (one of the Dutch dominies helped save Fr. Jogues from death at the hand of Indians in 1643)[2], as well as with Puritans, Lutherans, Anabaptists, and Jews.[3] The Lutherans worshipped with the Reformed, partook of Holy Communion, and had their children baptized by the Reformed clergy until about 1653, when they asked for their own services, which request was denied.[4] Stuyvesant, the governor, was less tolerant than his predecessors, and thus blemished the good record of the Dutch for toleration.

The first encounter with the Anglicans occurred when the English took over Nieuw Amsterdam in 1664, renamed it New York, and brought with them the English Church. The Dutch were promised freedom to practise their religion, inasmuch as the English recognised the Dutch Church to be a National Church like their own. But the attempt was made to establish the Church of England and win for it public financial support. This the large non-Anglican majority of the populace resisted; and, though "Secret Instructions" were sent by King James II to the New York governor, providing for the establishment of the Church of England, they were never effective.[5] When William III, a Dutchman, became King of England, the Dutch Church in New York realized that the time was ripe for them to act, and in 1696 they secured a royal charter which insured their continued existence. Trinity Church gained a charter in 1697, at which time they determined no longer to worship in the Dutch Church in the Fort, but to build their own building. Relations between the Dutch Reformed and the Episcopalians improved, and when the first minister of Trinity Church was inducted in 1697, the service took place in the Dutch Church in Garden Street, with two Dutch ministers taking a major role in the service.[6] Both the Dutch and English national churches held a special place in New York over against "dissenters" until the Revolution.

The Dutch Reformed had always had good relations with other Reformed and Presbyterian groups in New York, even if the English might regard such groups as dissenters. English Presbyterians were given religious freedom by the Dutch as soon as they requested it (1644/5).[7] In the 1680's many French Reformed Huguenots who fled at the revocation of the Edict of Nantes were welcomed by the Dutch and received into their membership. In 1709 large numbers of the Reformed people left the Palatinate in Germany because of war, starvation and religious persecution. They went first to England, where they were naturalized at the behest of Queen Anne. Some were sent on to Ireland, others to the Carolinas, but the largest group settled in the Hudson and Mohawk Valleys of New York, territory which the Dutch Reformed had already occupied. They were readily received as brethren into the Dutch Reformed Church.[8]

By the 1730's the Dutch Reformed Church had been in America for over a century, and many of its leaders were becoming restive under the government of the Classis of Amsterdam (Holland). This was particularly true of the younger clergy, and those who had been affected by the revivalism under the leadership of the Rev. T. J. Frelinghuysen (1691-1747), often regarded as the forerunner of the Great Awakening. The revivalist, or "new-school" party, especially wished to be able to ordain its own men, rather than send them to the Netherlands for education and ordination. One or two ordinations had occurred in America, but only by special permission of the Classis of Amsterdam and in extraordinary situations. In April 1738 a group of ministers met in New York and prepared eleven "Fundamental Articles" as a basis for their proposed "Coetus" under the Classis of Amsterdam. These articles were not approved by the Classis until 1747, the delay being chiefly due to fears that the American churches would soon demand complete independence. Some of the more conservative Dutch ministers in New York had encouraged that fear:

I am of the opinion that it will be more for an injury and confusion than for the gain, peace, and unity of our Reformed Low

Dutch Church, in case the thing goes on. Time and experience will show, and perhaps there will be a total defection from our dear Netherlandish Church (which may God forbid!) and then vale, patria, etc.[9]

Meanwhile, German congregations of the Reformed faith were being established in Pennsylvania under the leadership of John Philip Boehm, George Michael Weiss, and Michael Schlatter. Because the Palatinate Church did not have the financial resources to maintain church work overseas, they asked the Synod of South Holland of the Dutch Reformed Church to assume responsibility, which it did. Boehm had never been properly ordained, so he made application to the Classis of Amsterdam to have the Dutch ministers in New York ordain him. Approval was granted by the Classis, and in 1729 he was ordained in the Dutch Church of New York.[10] From this time until 1793 the German Reformed churches of Pennsylvania remained under the Reformed Church of Holland.

In 1743 the Synod of South Holland hit upon what seemed to them a happy solution to the problems of the immigrant churches in America which were under their care. Rather than grant the request of the German churches for a "Coetus" with a degree of independence under their supervision, they proposed that the German and Dutch Reformed Churches both unite with the Presbyterian Church, and form one strong Calvinist church in the colonies.[11] The Synod of North Holland, of which the Classis of Amsterdam was a member, agreed to the proposal, which was then sent to the German churches and the Presbyterian Synod via Peter Henry Dorsius, minister of the Dutch Reformed Church in Bucks County who was closely associated with Frelinghuysen and his revival.[12]

The proposal was well received by the Presbyterians of the Philadelphia Synod and by the Dutch Reformed of Bucks County, but the German Reformed churches absolutely refused to consider the proposal because of their attachment to their church constitution and their lack of ability to understand the English language. They also supposed they would lose the Heidelberg Catechism, and the Canons of Dort, if they joined the Presbyterians.[13] The Dutch Reformed of New York, the most conservative of all the Dutch churches, were also fearful of the proposed union because they believed the Presbyterians to have Arminian and Methodistic tendencies. This belief was founded on their acquaintance with the Presbyterians of the Synod of New York, with which the Tennent revivalist movement was affiliated. The Philadelphia Presbyterians, who had driven the revivalists out of their membership, were incensed at the charges of Arminianism, and also declared to the Synods of Holland that the Dutch and German churches would be able to keep the Heidelberg Catechism and the Canons of Dort.[14] In 1751 several Classes of the South Holland Synod overtured that the union be consummated, but that same year the North Holland Synod began to take seriously the New York Dutch charge of Arminianism in the "revivalist party," and lost interest in the proposal. The next year, the South Holland Synod also abandoned it, and the plan of union, with its possibilities of providing a united Presbyterian body for the American colonies, was lost. Briggs believed that the conservative Presbyterian party was responsible for the failure of this plan of union, but Good places the blame upon the revivalist parties.[15] Both are partially correct: Good no doubt correctly assumes that if there had been no revivalist party, union could have been accomplished; but Briggs is correct in seeing that, once there was a revivalist party, the conservatives blocked approval of union. The revivalists (Frelinghuysen and Tennent and their followers) were less rigid creedally, tended to blur denominational distinctions, worked well together, officiated in each others' churches, and were less bound to the traditions of their mother countries than were the orthodox.[16]

Shortly thereafter, the tension between Old School and New School, conservative and revivalist parties in the Dutch Reformed Church, became so severe that they broke apart as had the two Presbyterian wings somewhat earlier. The right to have a Coetus had finally been granted by the Classis of Amsterdam in 1747, nine years after the original request had been made. But the organization was not successful in holding the two groups together, and in 1754 the conservative, high-Calvinist group departed to form the *Conferentie,* leaving the Coetus in the hands of the revivalist, American, independent party. The actual cause for the division was the Coetus' request to the Classis of Amsterdam in 1754 that the American churches be formed into an independent Classis.[17] The Conferentie, led by the congregation in New York, was unsympathetic toward Frelinghuysen's desire to establish a college for Dutch Reformed students in America; it preferred, instead, to attach a Dutch Reformed professor of theology to the newly-established Kings College (Columbia) in New York.[18] Ironically, had this happened, the Reformed Church would have been *less* likely to remain independent from other churches than by following Frelinghuysen's plan.

The Classis of Amsterdam was unenthusiastic about both of the proposed schemes for educating young theologs in America: the proposal of some Conferentie folk, led by Dominie Ritzema of New York, to have a Dutch professor of divinity at Kings; and the determination of the Coetus group to establish a Dutch Reformed college, which would be for the Dutch alone.[19] The Classis proposed still a third alternative—that the Dutch Reformed join with those others who had founded the College of New Jersey (Princeton) in 1746, people whom the Classis understood to be the "purest Scotch Presbyterians."[20] This suggestion was rejected by Ritzema and his friends, partly no doubt because Ritzema hoped to be the Dutch professor named to Kings; it was also rejected by the members of the Coetus, because they forsaw, no doubt accurately, that union with the Presbyterians in the College of New Jersey would mean the eventual end of the Dutch Reformed Church as a separate entity.[21] The Rev. David Marinus, Coetus minister in Passaic, wrote:

We don't choose to have too near a connection with either (Presbyterians or Anglicans); but intend, please God, an academy of our own. . . . We have no business with their Colleges; . . . let every one provide for his own house.[22]

Though generally considered more cooperative with other denominations than the Conferentie, in this instance it was the Coetus which was less interested in cooperation than either the Conferentie or the Classis of Amsterdam.

Several events now occurred which resulted in the triumph of the Coetus' aims over those of the Conferentie. While the Anglicans in New York paid lip-service to the idea of a Dutch professor of divinity at Kings, there was no provision made for it when the charter was written. Furthermore, Ritzema's New York consistory disapproved of their minister's support of this scheme and made a formal complaint against him.[23] Meanwhile, it became apparent that the Coetus had the support of the majority of Dutch Reformed ministers in New York and New Jersey, and that this group was going to move ahead in organizing a Dutch Reformed college. Several unsuccessful attempts were made to gain a royal charter for a college before King George III finally granted one in 1766 through Governor Franklin of New Jersey.[24] While Rutgers University considers this its founding date, no instruction was begun until the granting of the second charter in 1770. The probable causes of the delay were the division in the Dutch Reformed Church, a lack of funds, and divided opinion as to the proposed location. In May 1771 it was finally decided that the college, to be called Queen's, should be located in New Brunswick, both because New Brunswick had provided a larger subscription for the college and because it was nearer than was Hackensack to the German Reformed Churches of Pennsylvania.[25]

Steps were now speedily taken to re-unite the Coetus and the Conferentie. Perhaps the successful reunion of Old Light and New Light Presbyterians in 1758 encouraged the Dutch. Already after the granting of the first charter of 1766, the Conferentie brethren had made overtures to the Coetus group, but nothing came of it.[26] Also in 1766, however, John Henry Livingston went to the Netherlands after graduation from Yale, in order to complete his theological education and be ordained. He took with him a scheme of union, which was soon approved by the Classis of Amsterdam. Upon his return to America in 1770, he became one of the ministers of the Church in New York, and within a year he had his Consistory send out an invitation to all Dutch Reformed Churches in New York and New Jersey. They were asked to meet in New York in October to consider a possible plan of union.[27] Thirty-four of the more than 100 churches were represented, including those of both parties as well as those who had remained neutral during the separation. A committee composed of four neutrals, four Conferentie men, and four Coetus representatives was appointed to study the plan, amend it if necessary, and recommend it to the body. This was done with little change in text, and the plan was unanimously approved by the Assembly. The plan provided for almost total autonomy for the American churches, as the Coetus had wished, but was sent to the Classis of Amsterdam for approval, in order to please the Conferentie. Approval came in a letter of congratulations from Amsterdam in January 1772, and by October of that year most of the American churches had ratified and placed themselves under the jurisdiction of the new judicatory created by the plan. The new organization was called the "General Body," with five subordinate "Particular Bodies;" this avoidance of normal terminology such as "synod" and "classis" was another attempt to please the Conferentie and disguise the *de facto* independence which the plan gave the American church. The only ties remaining with the church in the Netherlands were the common doctrinal and constitutional standards, and the agreement to submit all minutes of meetings of the judicatories to the mother Synod.[28] This was the first of only two unions accomplished by the Dutch Reformed in America; it was a re-union of sister congregations, having identical backgrounds, rather than a union of two denominations. It required a willingness to compromise on both sides, though the Coetus won on most counts. Without the leadership of John Henry Livingston, a neutral, it could not have been so smoothly accomplished, if at all; hence he is called the "Father of the Reformed Church."

III

The Struggle For Ethnic-Cultural Survival
(1771-1820)

The Reformed Church, having achieved *de facto* independence in 1771-2, spent the next half century achieving independence *de jure,* establishing the institutions she felt necessary to real independence and ethnic-cultural survival, preserving herself and her territory from encroachment by others, and seeking to extend herself into virgin western lands. These efforts were all related to each other, but dominating all other concerns was the desire of the church to have her own theological instruction; without it, a continued separate existence would not have been possible.

As early as 1772 and 1773, the matter of a theological professorate appeared on the agenda of the church's highest judicatory. The suggestion was made that, if New Brunswick were made the center of theological instruction, the professor of theology could double as president of Queen's College.[1] Unfortunately, the Revolutionary War was particularly hard on the Dutch Reformed Church, since most of the churches lay in battle areas—northern and central New Jersey, and the Hudson-Mohawk Valley. Also, most of the Dutch Reformed were patriots, who disliked English attempts to establish the Anglican church, who in General Synod called the Revolution "a just and necessary war,"[2] and who after the War unfrocked one of the ministers for Toryism.[3] (Andrew C. Leiby, in *The Revolutionary War in the Hackensack Valley*, claims that, in Bergen County, most Conferentie people were pro-British and most Coetus people anti-British.)[4] The British regarded the Dutch churches as fair game for burning, or for use as stables and barracks. By the end of the War, about half of the church buildings had been severely damaged or destroyed. Hence every effort of the church was required to restore normal religious life, and the professorate was neglected.

The year after war's end, 1784, the General Synod was at last able to establish theological instruction for the Reformed Church by appointing Dr. John H. Livingston as Professor of Sacred Theology in the City of New York.[5] In 1786 a second professor, the Rev. Hermannus Meyer, was appointed; and students, after studying with these two men, were considered ready for examinations for licensure and ordination. The question of the proper location for the theological school, and its relation to other colleges, was frequently raised. Queen's College was in financial trouble, so that her Trustees recommended union with Princeton.[6] When this proposal was turned down, another, also in 1793, suggested that the bachelor of arts degree be granted by Princeton, and the theological degree for both Dutch Reformed and Presbyterians be granted by Queen's.[7] Neither denomination approved of this plan. In 1794, it was proposed to move Queen's to Bergen (Jersey City), and the Divinity Hall to Flatbush.[8] Because living expenses were lower in Flatbush, Dr. Livingston did move there for a time, and taught in connection with Erasmus Hall Academy. Queen's was not moved, but collegiate instruction was suspended from 1795 to 1807.[9] During this period of inaction at Queen's, the Collegiate Church of New York once again raised the proposal that the theological professorate be attached to Columbia College, as provided for in the charter.[10] This was hastily declined by General Synod, stating that

They do not wish to blend their theological professorate with any other establishment not derived from the immediate authority of the Low Dutch Reformed Churches.[11]

With the re-opening of Queen's, Dr. Livingston was called to serve as President of the college and professor and head of the Theological School in 1810. Since that date, though General Synod appointed a committee to determine whether the Seminary should be in New York (1817),[12] both college and seminary have been firmly established in New Brunswick. A new constitution was adopted for the seminary in 1812, and the school was expanded to include four professors in 1815.[13]

Though the Dutch might not "wish to blend their theological professorate with any other establishment," they could not avoid contact with other denominations. In 1784 the General Synod appointed a committee of clergy to meet with a group of Presbyterian clergy to work out some sort of comity system, whereby the two denominations would not encroach on each other's territory.[14] This was in response to complaints from certain congregations. The members of this "comity" committee got on so well together that they proposed a plan of closer cooperation. General Synod agreed, provided there were "no intermixing or confounding of the two distinct ecclesiastical communions."[15] The fraternal correspondence between the two churches, and also the Associate Reformed Synod, continued in a somewhat haphazard fashion until 1797, when a plan of correspondence was to be drawn up. Presented to the General Synod of 1800, the plan proposed three kinds or degrees of association: a) intercommunion for members in good standing of the three churches; b) friendly interchange of ministers, both for occasional supply and for called and installed pastors; and c) exchange of delegates to the highest judicatories, with vote.[16] General Synod debated the plan for several days, considering both positive and negative resolutions, but ended without a decision. No more is heard of the plan, though correspondence between the churches continued. In 1816, a committee was appointed by General Synod to discuss unity with the Associate Reformed Synod alone.[17] The Synod of 1820 ratified the plan, and sent it to the classes for approval. A majority approved, as reported at the 1821 Synod—but unfortunately, word was received from the Associate Reformed Synod that they had turned it down.[18]

Much of the hesitance of the Dutch Reformed Church to enter into a pan-Presbyterian union may have come from the desire to unite with a church closer to them in doctrinal and geographic/ethnic background, the German Reformed churches in Pennsylvania. Many of the German Reformed churches located in Dutch Reformed areas, such as New York City and the Hudson-Mohawk Valley, attached themselves to the Dutch Reformed Synod as a matter of course.[19] Both churches had been under the Reformed Church of the Netherlands throughout the colonial period. In 1794 a committee was appointed, with Dr. Livingston as chairman, to open a friendly correspondence "and prosecute it to a union with the Reformed German churches of Pennsylvania."[20] Preachers for the German churches were secured from the German Synod in Pennsylvania.[21] Correspondence was maintained between the two denominations, and fraternal delegates exchanged. However, Dr. Livingston's committee did not succeed in "prosecuting it to a union." Hope revived in 1818, when word was received that the German Synod was interested in joining with the Dutch in the Seminary at New Brunswick—an aim in the minds of the Dutch when they established the seminary there. In 1820, however, it was learned that the Germans had laid plans to establish their own seminary.[22] One of the major problems at this time was the language dilemma—although the Dutch and German were closely related ethnically, the Dutch churches were by now all English-speaking, while the Germans were still using German even in their Synods, which complicated exchanges in both directions.

The Dutch Reformed Church was relatively unconcerned about relations with other churches at this time because she was a loosely organized and poorly integrated body herself. The original Plan of Union, while approved by the Church in the Netherlands, and by both Coetus and Conferentie in America, was binding upon local congregations only when they voted to subscribe to the plan. Concern was expressed about the "outstanding congregations" from time to time, that designation being one of the items on every year's agenda at Synod. The Church must encourage such congregations to join "to prevent the dangerous consequences of independency."[23] Albany, one of the most prominent of the churches, founded in 1642, did not join the union until 1785,[24] and Kingston, another historic and prominent church, held out until 1809.[25]

It was increasingly felt that the Plan of Union, which set up a "General Body" and five "Particular Bodies," was not an adequate system of church government. In view of American independence, the General Body was known as the "Synod" after 1785, while the particular bodies were called "Classes." In 1793, the Synod adopted its new Constitution and Liturgy, both in the English language. The Constitution was composed of the Ecclesiastical Rules of the Synod of Dort, along with Explanatory Articles for the American situation written by Dr. Livingston.[26]

A concern for the mission of the church, in the sense of going beyond present borders, was slow and gradual in development. The 1786 Synod appointed a committee to formulate plans for the "extension of the church." When they reported two years later, their concern was for new settlements—the people should be "formed into ecclesiastical societies," in order that they "would enlarge the body of our church."[27] To that end, congregations were asked to make voluntary collections which would be used to support ministers on the frontier. The committee might have left it at that, but in 1789 a medical doctor named Jacob Ginnings was recommended for ordination by some people in Hardy County, Virginia. The Synod was impressed by his knowledge and ability, and ordained him.[28] In 1790 mention is made of sending extension moneys to Kentucky, and in 1791 Dr. Ginnings complained because of lack of financial support.[29] Work was next begun along the Susquehannah, and in 1794 two men were appointed "missionaries for the purpose of extending the interest of our Dutch Church in the back country."[30] These projects in Virginia, Kentucky, and mid-Pennsylvania were all soon abandoned, but an extension project in Upper Canada (Ontario) along the St. Lawrence captured the interest of the church for twenty years (1800-20). The Rev. Robert MacDowell established a score of churches, and wished to organize a Classis, but no additional missionaries could be found, so the work and the churches were turned over to the Presbyterian Church in Canada.[31]

While the story of cooperative mission beginnings on the denominational level will be told in the next chapter, the first voluntary missionary societies involving Dutch Reformed individuals in interdenominational activity begin during this period. In 1796 members of Presbyterian, Associate Reformed (United Presbyterian), Dutch Reformed and Baptist churches in the City of New York founded the New York Missionary Society to "propagate the glorious gospel of Christ, in places which are destitute of it."[32] Persons, and congregations, could be admitted "from all religious denominations indiscriminately."[33] It was in theory a world missionary society, for "it will make no difference whether they (are) gathered from the banks of the Mississippi, the Gambia, or the Ganges."[34] Leading laymen and clergy of the Dutch Reformed Church were directors and officers of the society, including Dr. Livingston as vice-president. Among the early missionaries supported by the group were the Rev. Joseph Bullen of Vermont, sent to the Chickasaw Indians of Georgia; John Sergeant, missionary to the Stockbridge Indians; and "Paul," an Indian preacher on Long Island.[35] The society made it clear that, while "the hearty concurrence of Christians of different denominations . . . will be a token for good," it was not a political combination, nor a step toward church union. "We disclaim all intention of interfering, directly or indirectly, with the internal arrangements or other peculiarities of any Christian denomination."[36] A similar society, the Northern Missionary Society, was organized by representatives of the same denominations at Lansingburgh in upstate New York in 1797. They also concentrated on work among the American Indians.[37]

The New York and Northern Missionary Societies, while ostensibly world-wide in scope, were supported only by individuals and congregations in the local areas. In 1816 the General Assembly of the Presbyterian Church invited the corresponding Dutch Reformed and Associate Reformed judicatories to send representatives to a meeting at which a joint society for foreign missions would be established.[38] The Constitution, approved in 1817, stated the object of the United Foreign Missionary Society to be "to spread the gospel among the Indians of North America, the inhabitants of Mexico and South America, and in other portions of the heathen and anti-Christian world."[39] Other churches were welcome to join with these three; and individuals could become members by paying a $3 annual fee. While having denominational backing, it was another voluntary society with individual memberships the main source of support. The Honorable Stephen van Rensselaer, a Dutch Reformed layman, was the first president, and Dr. Livingston was also vice-president of this society.[40] A young Dutch Reformed doctor in New York City, calling one day in 1819 on a patient, read a tract of the society called "The Conversion of the World, or the Claims of Six Hundred Millions." He borrowed it, re-read it, and cried, "Lord, what wilt thou have me to do?" An inner voice said "Go and preach the gospel to the heathen."[41] The doctor was Dr. John Scudder, who went that year to India, under the American Board of Commissioners for Foreign Missions. He was ordained by an ecumenical group in Ceylon in 1821 (Baptists, Methodists, and Congregationalists), and later founded the (Dutch Reformed) Arcot Mission.[42] He was the ancestor of a great missionary dynasty, including several sons and grandchildren (among them Dr. Ida Scudder) who gave a total of over 1000 years of missionary service.

It is to Dr. Livingston that much of the credit must be given for stimulating interest in missions both foreign and domestic. As noted, he served on the boards of two voluntary missionary societies. He preached sermons on missions which received wide distribution. In one of these, "The Everlasting Gospel," he saw the modern mission movement as the prelude to the binding of the anti-Christ and the coming of the millenium, according to his reckonings due in 2000 A.D. This gave an urgency to mission activity.[43] In 1811 he led in the founding of the Berean Society (since 1820 the Society of Inquiry) at New Brunswick Seminary, "to diffuse among ourselves a zeal for the missionary cause."[44]

This first half-century of independence was, as we have seen, one of securing and strengthening the organizational life of the denomination and her institutions. As the period began, the Dutch Reformed Church was one of the half-dozen or so leading denominations, and the possibilities of the new country must have seemed limitless. Hence there was little compulsion toward union with others. But the rising interest in missions to people different from themselves did result in cooperative work on the individual and also on the denominational level. There was a recognition of the common quality of their Christian faith with others, but also a desire to preserve newly-won independence and what they regarded as a unique historic tradition.

IV

Joint Action in Missions, Federations and Alliances (1820-1885)

United Work in China, India, and Japan

The middle period of the nineteenth century (from about 1820 to 1885) saw far-reaching changes taking place in the life of the Dutch Reformed Church in her relations with other Christian bodies. It was during this period that she established her reputation as a great missionary church, but her approach to the overseas mission underwent several dramatic shifts during this sixty-five year period. Four stages are evident:

a) Continuation of activity through voluntary societies;

b) Work through the American Board of Commissioners for Foreign Missions;

c) Efforts entirely on her own;

d) United missions and native churches with those of similar theology.

After the initial rash of new voluntary missionary societies in the early nineteenth century, a gradual process of consolidation took place. The New York Missionary Society, a local group dominated by Presbyterians and Dutch Reformed, united in 1821 with the national United Foreign Missionary Society of similar background.[1] This larger society in turn voted, and its constituent denominations approved, to unite with the American Board of Commissioners for Foreign Missions in 1826.[2] The approach remained that of the voluntary society until 1831, when the Rev. Wm. McMurray, chairman of the General Synod's Missions committee asked Synod whether they, as a denomination, would entertain the subject of foreign missions at all, and if so, whether they wanted an entirely independent operation or an effort "more or less combined with others."[3] McMurray advocated a connection with the American Board, which would leave to the Dutch church the selection of missionaries, the choice of missionary stations, and the direction of organization of the new churches. A committee worked out such an agreement, which allowed the Dutch church to profit by the experience and know-how of the American Board without giving up control. Dr. John Scudder of Ceylon (and later of India) and the Rev. David Abeel of China, both Reformed Church men under the American Board, were supported by the Reformed Church after this 1832 concordat was approved by Synod.[4]

Four years later the first proposal to withdraw from the American Board came before Synod, but it was pointed out to the church by the Missions chairman that "we had sought this connection and the American Board has given us privileges which no other denomination . . . enjoyed,"[5] so no further action was taken. Abeel established a mission in Borneo in 1836, and five missionary families joined him there under the American Board in succeeding years. The Dutch Government was less than cooperative, however, and in 1842 Abeel moved to Amoy, China, where the bulk of the Borneo mission joined him in 1844.[6] The Scudder mission in India was so successful that in 1854 the Classis of Arcot was formed under the Particular Synod of New York.[7]

The Dutch Reformed Church, after having worked overseas for nearly a quarter-century under the American Board with special privileges, became somewhat restive in regard to the arrangement. A whole packet of letters from clergy, asking separation from the American Board, reached Synod in 1856. Synod was impressed by the Reformed Church's successes in India and China, but there were weightier reasons given for separation: a desire to put responsibility squarely upon the denomination; the church was ready to do its own work, and capable of it; there was a growing disinclination toward voluntary societies, and a greater emphasis on ecclesiastical responsibility; and independent missions would complete the full range of church activity. In tones reminiscent to us of Robert Frost's "Mending Wall," the chairman concluded, "It does not follow that because a man keeps up good enclosures . . . therefore he is estranged from his neighbours."[8] So, in 1857, an early ecumenical venture ended as the Dutch Church and the American Board parted amicably, with the church firmly stating it had no dissatisfaction with the Board's work.[9]

Then followed a brief period in which, theoretically at least, the Reformed Church was doing her mission work alone—theoretically, because although that was the aim and intent of the Synod and the church at home, the missionaries realized its impracticability. Dr. John V. N. Talmage, leading missionary and "bishop" of the Amoy Mission, wrote to the General Synod in 1856, asking for permission to organize some kind of ecclesiastical assembly which would em-

brace both the Dutch Reformed and English Presbyterian missionaries and churches in Amoy. They had grown up together, had
always cooperated closely, and the Chinese neither recognized any
distinction between the two nor could express any such difference
in their language.[10] The General Synod of 1857, involved in pulling
out of the cooperative work with the American Board, was not
favorably inclined to this proposal. Dr. Talbot W. Chambers of the
Collegiate Church, chairman of the Committee on Foreign Missions,
spoke the mind of the church when he stated that they expected the
converts to be "an integral part of our church," and that permission
would be given to form a Classis of Amoy, under the Synod of
Albany.[11]

Talmage wrote a letter of protest, stating that to form a Dutch
Reformed Classis in China would break up an already united Reformed-Presbyterian church in existence there. Synod did not reply.
Meanwhile, the Mission advanced and in 1862 formed an organization called the "Tai-hoey of Amoy," translated as "The Great
Presbyterian and Classical Council of Amoy."[12] They then reported
to the Presbyterian Church of England as the Presbytery of Amoy
and to the Reformed Church as the Classis of Amoy. Dr. Isaac
Ferris, Mission Secretary, brought this to the attention of the Synod
of 1863, stating that it was contrary to the 1857 Synod action, and
asking whether or not the Synod intended to stand by that action,
inasmuch as "this Synod, in its action on this case, will decide for
all its missions, and in all time, on what principles their missionaries
shall act."[13] Talmage, home from China, moved that the present
arrangement be approved. Dr. Chambers argued with eloquent
provincialism against the motion:

A 'self-regulating' Classis is a thing which has never been heard
of in the Dutch Church since that Church had a beginning. It is
against every law, principle, canon, example, and precedent in our
books . . . How can we violate our own order? . . . When we made
a compact with the American Board, one essential feature of the
plan was that we should have 'an ecclesiastical organization' of our
own. Without this feature that plan would never have been adopted;
and the apprehension that there might be some interference with
this cherished principle was at least one of the reasons why the
plan . . . was at length abrogated. . . . It was my privilege to draw up
the report on the subject. . . . [Separate organization] is our
settled, irreversible policy. . . . We are acting for all time. . . . How
can our disapproval of the mongrel Classis mar the peace of the
Amoy brethren?[14]

Synod defeated Talmage's motion, and voted that while much must
be left to the missionaries' discretion, "The wish and expectation of
this Synod is to have their action conform, as soon as may be, to the
resolution of 1857."[15] In the meantime, the Presbyterian Church of
England approved the arrangement, and Talmage again wrote a
long letter pointing out the need for an indigenous church and the
impossibility of being an organic part of the church in America.
The Synod of 1864 received notice from the Amoy missionaries that
they would all resign if the issue were forced, and therefore voted
a final reluctant motion: "the brethren there are allowed to defer
the formation of a Classis of Amoy until, in their judgment, such a
measure is required by the wants and desires of the Churches
gathered by them from among the heathen."[16] Thus, Chambers and
others notwithstanding, Synod did not determine policy "for all
time;" the Mission determined it, and Synod later realized the
Mission's wisdom. A later writer said, "The question was never
broached again. The strongest opponents then are the warmest
friends of union and autonomy now."[17] A major ecumenical break-
through had occurred, which was to set the future pattern of all
mission activity overseas of the Reformed Church.

The period of independent work in India was longer than in
China, though not because of the wishes of missionaries there. The
seven Scudder brothers, sons of the original Dr. Scudder, formed
the backbone of the Classis of Arcot which had been founded in
1854.[18] The General Synod of 1867 received a communication from
that Classis, asking permission to cooperate in a convention of all
the Presbyterian bodies active in India to consider the "expediency
of uniting Presbyterians generally in one General Assembly in
India."[19] It would seem that the General Synod had learned something from their experience in China, for they voted

That this Synod sees no reasons why the missionaries of our
Church in India should not hold themselves open to any suggestions
which may be made on the subject of Presbyterial relations between
the several mission churches in India; but that the whole matter be
entrusted to the discretion of our missionaries, with the understanding that they are to commit themselves to no practical scheme,
without the formal approbation of the Synod.[20]

Movement toward a united Presbyterian body in India was very
slow. In 1874 the Synod again received word of some kind of
presbyterial confederation underway, and again expressed their

approval, so long as it did not conflict with relations between missionaries and the home Board.[21] The next year, in discussing closer relations with the Presbyterian Church in the United States, the Reformed Church made an unambiguous statement of its intent to aid only in the establishment of united indigenous churches:

And this agreement (for cooperation) is made not only for the purpose of expressing, as it does, the confidence which these two American churches have in each other, but chiefly with the view of contributing to the establishment in each mission country of a National Church that shall grow from its own root.[22]

The fact that the first union in India was delayed until the turn of the century was not due to the reluctance of the missionaries and Synod of the Reformed Church, but to the other bodies involved.

A new mission was established in Japan by the Reformed Church in 1859. Initially it too was an independent operation. Requests had been made, immediately after the signing that year of the Japanese-American Treaty, for missionaries to be sent to Japan by the Boards of the Reformed Church, the Protestant Episcopal Church, and the Presbyterian Church. The Reformed Board sent three men and their families (Dr. D. Simmons, Dr. Samuel R. Brown, and the Rev. Guido Verbeck), the Episcopalians two, and the Presbyterians one.[23] Soon after, in 1862, the Rev. James H. Ballagh joined the Reformed mission, and became pastor of the first church in Japan, "The Church of Christ in Japan," in Yokohama, in 1872.[24] This church was organized on an independent basis, inasmuch as it was the only church in the country, but the situation made the General Synod uneasy. They recognized it as a true church of Jesus Christ, and re-invoked the regulation of 1864 then applied to the Amoy mission "as far as the principle therein stated is applicable to this case."[25] The principle mentioned was that formation of a classis might be delayed until the churches there desired one. This opened the way for the formation in 1877 of The United Church of Our Lord Jesus Christ in Japan, by the Reformed Church, the Presbyterian Church in the U. S. A., and the United Presbyterian Church of Scotland. In 1885 the Southern Presbyterians and German Reformed also joined the others to form a new "United Church of Christ in Japan," with five presbyteries and forty-five churches.[26] Thus, by the end of this period, China and Japan had united churches, and approval had been given for one in India.

Voluntary Societies & Alliances

Though the Reformed Church had become a parent of several "younger churches" by the end of the century, voluntary benevolent societies continued to be popular with members of the Reformed Church and with the General Synod itself. The American Bible Society, one of the oldest, was founded in 1816 in the Garden St. Reformed Church of New York City. No mention is made of the Bible Society until 1829, but thereafter it is commended to the members of the church with great regularity.[27] The American Tract Society (1825) was another popular charity. In 1833 the General Synod listed seven societies for which it urged support: The American Bible Society, The American Tract Society, The American Seaman's Friend Society, The A. B. C. F. M., The American Colonization Society (trying to transport American Negroes to Africa), The American Sunday School Union, and The American Temperance Society.[28] These societies were popular with individual Protestants of most denominational backgrounds. Some of the more unusual groups have disappeared, but the Tract and Bible Societies are still supported to-day by the Reformed and other churches.

The Reformed Church also participated, as the century moved on, in the development of alliances and federations. The earliest such group to attract her attention was the Evangelical Alliance, founded in London in 1846. In arguing for a delegation from the Reformed Church, advocates quoted John 17.[29] A Reformed Church delegation attended, and encouraged Reformed Church members to join the Alliance when an American section was established in 1854. This Alliance developed a creedal statement of a conservative Protestant nature, which represented the theological position of many denominations of the time. It stressed unity for evangelical Protestants, but it was still in format a "voluntary, irresponsible body, amenable to no ecclesiastical organization," as the General Synod complained.[30] Certain critics felt that it was too largely an anti-Roman body, based on individual piety rather than real concern for church union, and thus moving in the wrong direction.[31] The Reformed Church lost interest in the Alliance as other concerns arose.

It is difficult to determine just what the Reformed Church desired in the way of federation or alliance in the mid-nineteenth century and soon after. The Presbyterian General Assembly proposed in 1847 that a conference be held to work out a suitable plan of intercourse between themselves, the Associate Reformed Presbyterians, the Reformed Presbyterians, the Associate Presbyterians, and the Dutch and German Reformed churches. Synod voted to send delegates, and a report on the "Convention of Representatives of Presbyterian Denominations" was made two years later. It was resolved to work for union among the bodies represented, to cooperate in missions, ministerial exchange, correspondence, and further conventions.[32] Nothing further is heard of this attempt at closer relations. In 1865 another call came from the Presbyterians for an alliance, this time of all evangelical churches, to express "our desire for fellowship and more vigorous cooperation for the defence of Protestant Christianity against the encroachments of the Roman Catholic Church."[33] This seemed too negative a basis for any alliance; Synod asked whether this would not give it the "appearance of religious persecution."[34] The Synod was, however, willing to appoint a committee to promote the positive tasks of the Protestant community. "Leaving the past to bury its dead, the Evangelical Church is looking to the future."[35] Apparently the Reformed Church's suggestion was not agreeable to the Presbyterians, because the committee appointed does not again appear. In 1868 the Reformed Church took the initiative, stating that "whereas the doctrinal and governmental system of the Reformed Church is broad and Catholic," it would ask other denominations to join a "National Council of Evangelical denominations," to promote, "*not* organic, but fraternal union."[36] Many denominations responded to the invitation, and a body was formed, sometimes called the "National Evangelical Council," and at other times "The National Council of Evangelical Churches."[37] Once again, the attempt was abortive, with no further meetings.

The Rev. B. M. Schmucker, a Lutheran pastor, proposed in a "Fraternal Appeal" of 1873 that the denominations whose members had been interested in the Evangelical Alliance, form a "voluntary advisory confederation," to promote harmony, free sacramental (inter)communion and recognition. The Reformed Church, never too enthusiastic about the Evangelical Alliance, and always more inclined toward programs limited to Presbyterian bodies, declined support for this effort, on the grounds that the diversity among those denominations would cause more division than union.[38] This was the last proposal within the present period for broad interdenominational alliance.

The same year Schmucker issued his appeal the Presbyterians had another idea for federation within the Reformed family, this to be on a world-wide basis rather than simply American. The Reformed Church sent delegates to a conference in New York in December

1874, at which a 22-point program for the proposed alliance was formulated. Only churches whose creed was "in conformity with the *consensus* of the Reformed Church" would be admitted. It would work for religious liberty, for instruction in the Scriptures, preservation of the Sabbath, opposition to infidelity, etc.[39] The Constitution of the "Presbyterian Alliance," as it was first called, was adopted at a meeting in London in July 1875, and the first General Council met in Edinburgh in 1876. The Reformed Church in America has continued its membership in this oldest of the world confessional alliances, which is today known as "The Alliance of Reformed Churches Throughout the World Holding the Presbyterian Order."

Secession, Union, & Secession Again

Numerous as the proposed and actual federations and alliances were in which the Reformed Church was involved, equally numerous if not more so were the attempts at union with another denomination or denominations during this period. Only one union was consummated, that with a fellow Dutch Reformed body; and the story of that union is interwoven with the history of the three secessions from the Reformed Church which also occurred in this period. In 1822 a small number of ministers and churches, under the leadership of Dr. Solomon Froeligh, seceded from the Reformed Church and called themselves the "True Reformed Dutch Church in the United States of America." They charged the Reformed Church with false doctrine, and with failure to remain true to the theological standards of the church. Their main accusation was that the Reformed Church held Hopkinsian doctrines of "New England Theology." Among these were a denial of the total corruption of human nature and original sin, a denial of limited atonement, an affirmation of man's natural ability to do good, and the teaching that all sin consists in selfishness.[40] The immediate cause for the accusation was the failure of General Synod to unfrock a Mr. Ten Eyck, minister in an upstate village, for ambiguity about traditional Reformed doctrine. Jacob Brinkerhoff, who was present at the organizational meeting of the True Dutch Church in 1822, in his "History" of that church, maintained that Dr. Froeligh seceded because he had not been named professor of theology at the seminary, though the Synod had previously made him a lector in theology.[41] He gathered together several other ministers, all of whom had at one time or another been suspended from the ministry. Soon after organization, they excommunicated the whole Reformed

Church, and were extremely antagonistic toward all other denominations. After a few years, one half of the church excommunicated the other half. A later writer described the True Dutch group as a "pietistic, Labadistic, and Antinomian schism," which overemphasized predestination.[42]

In 1847 another body of seceders came to the attention of the General Synod. "A body of Pilgrims has reached our shores from Holland," Synod was told, and a request for aid was made. These new immigrants had seceded from the Reformed Church of the Netherlands (the State Church) in 1834 because of alleged doctrinal laxity in the mother church, and because that church since 1816 had been governed by the King through a small governmental department. Most of these immigrants settled in Michigan, and formed a "Classis of Holland" there in 1848. The Reformed Church, which had had little success in extending the church in the West, saw this as an opportunity for westward expansion. In an 1848 Domestic Missions report, the Secretary said, "Other denominations are using active measures to bring them under their influence, while we, who are of the same origin, springing from the same branch of the Reformation . . . are doing nothing but exposing them to be swallowed up by men of every name and every creed."[43] That autumn the Classis of Holland was invited by the Reformed Church to attend the Synod meetings, and in 1849 Dr. Isaac Wyckoff of Albany visited them on behalf of the Board of Domestic Missions. The Classis prepared a request for admission into the Reformed Church, a document with an ecumenical flavor:

Considering the precious and blessed unity of the Church of God and the plainly expressed will of our Saviour that all should be one, and also the need which the separate parts have of one another, and especially remembering how small and weak we ourselves are, therefore, our hearts have longed for intercourse with the precious Zion of God ever since our feet first pressed the shores of this New World . . . all God's children, of whatever denomination, are dear to us; but in the management and care of our own religious affairs we feel more at home where we find our own standards of faith and principles of church government . . . We have, therefore, resolved to send one of our brethren, Rev. A. C. Van Raalte, a minister of the Church of God, as a delegate to your church Judicatory, which is soon about to meet in Albany or vicinity. We authorize him in our name to give and to ask all necessary information which can facilitate the desired union.[44]

The Synod of 1850 voted to receive the Classis into the membership of the Reformed Church, a step which was to give her a foothold in the West, but which was also to complicate her ecumenical relations in the future.

While the bulk of the leadership of the new Dutch colony in Michigan had the ecumenical spirit of the document just quoted, the Minutes of the Classis of Holland (1848-1858) show that there were others who were seceders by nature. As early as 1853 one of the congregations seceded, and its minister was deposed by the Classis.[45] An elder, G. J. Haan, constantly agitated the church, and was opposed to union with the Reformed Church. He accused her of heresy, and in support of his charges quoted attacks which the members of the True Reformed Dutch Church had made upon the Reformed Church when they seceded a quarter-century before.[46] In 1857, Haan was instrumental in having four congregations secede, giving as reasons: a) the use of hymns; b) inviting members of other churches to the Lord's Supper; c) neglecting to preach the Catechism; d) use of religious publications of other churches; e) regarding secession as not strictly necessary; and f) the alleged fact that the Rev. Mr. Wyckoff of Albany had given them permission to leave if they wanted to.[47] Van Raalte, the leading minister in the colony, answered all charges and indicated that they were the result of a mixture of ignorance, sectarianism, and "a trampling under foot of the brethren."[48] Haan later returned to the Reformed Church, then later seceded again. The little church he started, which called itself the Christian Reformed Church, survived the first decades of its life only with great difficulty.

About a decade after Haan's secession, however, a new agitation began in the western section of the Reformed Church, which was to be the salvation of the seceder church. An ex-Mason held a series of meetings in western Michigan in which he attacked secret societies. He may have been a left-over from the anti-Masonic agitation of an earlier generation. His activities led to overtures to the General Synod in 1868 from the Classes of Holland and Wisconsin, asking that Synod express its disapproval of the Order of Freemasons, "in order that the moral power of our whole Reformed Church may be against a great and growing evil."[49] Synod stated simply that it did not consider it proper to express its opinion in the case, hoping that the issue could be settled locally. But further communications came from the same classes in 1869, and a special committee was appointed on the subject. Reporting in 1870, this committee re-affirmed what the earlier Synod said, indicating in addition that while they believed secret societies were unnecessary, for consistories to exclude Masons would be to set up a new and unauthorized test of membership for the Christian church.[50] While this quieted discussion of the subject at Synod for some years, it remained a subject of discussion in the West, for in 1880 all four Classes of the Synod of Chicago, and the Synod itself, petitioned General Synod to oppose Free-Masonry actively on the grounds of its being anti-republican, anti-Christian, and anti-Reformed.[51] Synod, while appreciating the problem faced where anti-Masonic agitation existed, and while stating that no member of the church might join any anti-Christian society, again refused to set up any new test of membership in the church, and urged patience and forbearance.[52] The next year further overtures appeared from the same classes, and Synod's patience was tried so severely that it simply re-affirmed its previous actions and regarded the case as closed.[53] It was anything but closed, however; that year a number of churches in the Synod of Chicago seceded over the Masonry question, reducing the membership of the Classis of Holland alone by over 800 members.[54] These churches shortly joined up with the 1857 seceders, and later were also joined by the remaining remnant of the True Reformed Dutch Church, the resulting body being known today as the Christian Reformed Church.

The German Reformed Church

The Church with which the Dutch Reformed had the most continuing concern for closer relations and eventual union was its twin sister, the German Reformed Church. As noted earlier, both churches were daughters of the Reformed Church in the Netherlands, and it was primarily the language problem that kept them separate in the eighteenth and early nineteenth centuries. In 1834 the fraternal delegate from the German Synod to the Dutch made a plea for missionary assistance in reaching the destitute German immigrants in the West, particularly in the Alleghenies. The Dutch voted to help their German brethren by sending missionaries, and training those who could use the German language.[55]

In 1842, a century after union with the German Church had first been proposed, a committee was once again appointed to attempt closer relations with the German Church. This was particularly desirable, the Rev. John Knox said, because "the Dutch Reformed Church is confined within comparatively narrow geographical limits, is compact, and with her College and Theological seminary in successful operation . . . has the prospect of a redundant ministry." On the other hand, the German Church had a ministry "entirely too few in number to meet her urgent need."[56] In spite of all the two churches had in common, the joint Committee did "not feel that the condition of the two churches would warrant at present an entire amalgamation into one," but they did propose a Triennial Convention, with twelve delegates each from the Dutch and the two German synods. This convention was to be advisory only, but the three synods would try to work together in the Western mission field, and the Dutch would assist with surplus ministers.[57]

The plan for a triennial convention was approved by both the Dutch and German Synods, delegates were appointed, and the convention was held at Harrisburg, Pa., in August 1844. A general review of the work and problems of each church was presented at the convention, and a keynote sermon was preached by Dr. John W. Nevin, entitled "Catholic Unity." This sermon spoke of the Holy Catholic Church as being one in potential, but that the task of the churches was to help actualize this ideal by healing her visible divisions.[58] To that end the committee on action, under Nevin's chairmanship, proposed the following:

1. That the licentiates of the respective Synods . . . shall be considered as candidates in all the churches represented in this convention . . . .
2. That a correspondence be maintained between the students of the seminaries of each church, to cultivate reciprocal affection, and to awaken a mutual interest in the rising ministry of the respective bodies.
3. That the system of instruction in the seminaries . . . be conformed to each other as nearly as may be . . . .
4. That there should be as near an agreement as possible in the liturgy and form of worship in the churches of the different bodies represented.
5. That vigorous efforts be made by the Dutch Reformed Church to extend her missionary operations in the destitute parts of the German Reformed Church . . . [and that they join whichever denomination was nearest].[59]

These proposals were approved by both denominations, and plans were laid for a second convention in 1847.

Meanwhile, however, Dr. Nevin was joined on the Mercersburg (German Reformed) faculty by Dr. Philip Schaf (later Schaff), and these two men were to be responsible for the "Mercersburg Theol-

ogy" which, ironically, prevented the implementation of the above
proposals of Nevin's committee. Nevin had earlier become known
for his opposition to such revivalistic measures as the "anxious
bench," in which he would find agreement among the Dutch Reformed. But in 1845 Nevin was brought up on charges of holding
false views of the Lord's Supper. His views were classical Calvinism,
in contrast to the prevailing Zwinglianism in both German and
Dutch churches. Though Nevin was vindicated, even the hint of a
divergent theology was enough to scare the Classis of Bergen of the
Dutch Church. When that Classis' communications came before
General Synod, Synod's committee very delicately suggested that
the Dutch Church should not meddle in the German Church's
affairs, nor disrupt the newly-blooming romance between the two;
yet concern for "orthodoxy" impelled them to set up a committee
to discuss the matter with the Germans.[60] At the 1847 Synod attention was called to the fact that Dutch Reformed men interested in
serving the German church had not found pulpits there, none of the
other aims of the Triennial Convention had been achieved, and
consideration should be given to its termination.[61] Delegates were
appointed, and the convention held, but the 1848 Synod voted to
discontinue this close relationship.

Up to this point the Dutch Reformed objections to "Mercersburg
Theology" simply revealed that church's misunderstanding of its
own Calvinistic heritage, and the blame for dissolution of the Triennial Convention rests upon the Dutch. In 1850 the Dutch delegate
to the German Synod spoke with warm approval of the German
Church's awakening interest in the Liturgy, always a matter of
pride for the Dutch.[62] But by 1852 Nevin had revealed that his
interest in liturgy required that he consider pre-Reformation sources
as seriously as the mother Palatinate liturgy.[63] Also, Nevin's views
of the church led him into a flirtation with Rome and caused him to
resign his professorship. This was a period called by Nichols and
others "Nevin's five years of dizziness."[64] At the 1852 Dutch Synod,
its fraternal delegates to the German Synod reported on that Synod's
refusal to accept Nevin's resignation. This the Dutch interpreted as
a synodical endorsement "of the Romanizing tendency" of his opinions which set a "perilous course" for that church. Synod voted to
reduce its representation at the German Synod from two to one; but
the German Synod felt "aggrieved" at the above remarks about
them, stating that the Dutch delegates' remarks of the previous
year "with a single exception, do not contain a single statement in
accord with actual facts."[65] This charge in turn angered the Dutch

Synod, which voted its opposition to the erroneous doctrines of the Church of Rome, its protest against "all those sentiments of a Romanizing character . . . technically known as the 'Mercersburg Theology'," and its suspension of the correspondence between the two churches as a protest against Romanizing tendencies in the German church.[66]

Nothing further is heard of the German Reformed Church in official Dutch annals for a decade, except for the request of the North Carolina Classis of the German Church to be accepted into the Dutch Church (1855) "because of the innovations of Drs. Nevin and Schaff."[67] The Dutch Church was favorable until they discovered that the Germans approved of slave-holding, which led them to refuse the request.[68] Dr. Joseph Berg, one of Nevin's chief opponents, moved from the German to the Dutch Church, and continued to attack Nevin in the *Protestant Review* (which he edited) and the *Christian Intelligencer*. But by 1863 Schaff had left Mercersburg for New York, Nevin had become inactive, and Mercersburg was closed because of the Civil War.[69] Berg, too, had quieted down, and the Reformed Church decided it was time to re-open the fraternal correspondence with the German brethren. Of particular interest to both churches was the tercentenary that year of the Heidelberg Catechism.

In 1870-71 the German Reformed Synod of the West, and the Classis of North Carolina, again asked to join the Dutch Church. The slavery issue was now dead, but the Dutch discovered that both of these German groups really belonged to the German Reformed Synod, and acceptance of them would be an unfraternal act to that body. In 1873 when study was made of relations with various Presbyterian bodies, Synod's chairman, while indicating his preference for union with the German Reformed Church, asked and got the appointment of a committee to determine whether that body, the Northern Presbyterians, or the Southern Presbyterians should be approached for closer relations. Because of that committee's report (see below), relations with the German Reformed Church at the end of the period were cordial, with the Mercersburg controversy receding into the background, but with actual union nowhere in sight.

The Presbyterian Church in the United States

The committee appointed by General Synod made contacts with the German Reformed, Northern and Southern Presbyterians dur-

ing the year 1873-4, and reported back a major interest in the
Presbyterian Church, U. S. (South). This was something of a surprise to the Synod, which by a close vote (58-52) sustained the
committee's belief that the Dutch Church was "not ready to unite"
with the Northern Presbyterians. It was a surprise also because of
the Dutch Reformed Church's earlier opposition to slavery. But, of
course, now the War was over, slavery was abolished, and the
Reformed Church was one of the first northern denominations to
recognize the Presbyterian Church U. S., suggesting in 1870 that
they work together in extending the church among the "Freedmen."[70]
Thus some preparation had been made for the "intimate cooperative
alliance" which was now proposed by the committee for the two
churches. After a preamble which stated each church's recognition
of the other's doctrinal standards, similarity of government, confidence in each other, and desire for unity, the concrete proposals
for cooperation were as follows: a) ministerial and elder delegates
to be sent to each other's highest judicatory; b) vacant churches to
be free to call men from either church; c) churches free to belong
to either body, depending on their location; d) seminary students
from both churches to be equal in both churches; e) union of
boards of foreign and domestic missions, and publications. These
provisions, it was believed, would provide "a union, not organic, but
nevertheless a union real and practical."[71]

These proposals were spelled out in fuller detail the following
year. The publishing house of each church was to be agent and
depository for the other's publications as well as its own, and together
they were to prepare a children's paper. The Reformed churches
were asked to make financial contributions to the home missionary
work of the Southern Church among the Negroes. Foreign missions
in contiguous areas were to be formed into united churches, in
order to encourage growth of a native Christian church. Missionaries
from either church would be able to serve in either church, without
transferring their membership. Seminaries were to instruct theologs
about both churches' missions. Funds of either church's Board of
Education could be used to support students at seminaries of either
church. Annual reports of all agencies were to be exchanged. The
General Synod proceeded to adopt this plan.[72]

The plan at first appeared to have brought into being a "union
real and practical," if not organic. In the first couple of years after
its adoption, the Reformed Church voted to raise money for a
mission to Negroes in North Carolina, and urged the financial
support of Tuscaloosa (Ala.) Institute (later Stillman College), a

Southern Presbyterian school for Negroes. Contributions were not large, however, and real "engagement" between the two churches did not occur.[73] In 1879, a proposal was made that the Dutch Church keep up its fraternal correspondence with other churches by letter rather than by delegate, with the exception that "our relations to the Presbyterian Church (South) are so intimate and peculiar that it is necessary that there should be an annual interchange."[74] Five years later, however, the Southern Presbyterians also received only a letter;[75] and from then until very recently, no more was heard of the "union, not organic, but nevertheless . . . real and practical."

The Reformed Church was a great believer in correspondence with other churches, even if she shied away from union. All through this period she remained in correspondence with the Northern Presbyterian Church, though relations were plagued with local comity difficulties. Correspondence by delegate was also maintained with the United Presbyterians and Reformed Presbyterians, until one year the Reformed delegate was refused communion at the latter Assembly.[76] Correspondence by letter was kept in rather sporadic fashion with Reformed churches in other countries—the mother Netherlands Reformed Church, the Reformed Church of France, the Waldensian Church, the Dutch Reformed Church of South Africa, the Presbyterian Church in Canada, and others. Beyond Reformed circles, a delegate was exchanged with the Evangelical Lutheran Church for a number of years. Only one church was rebuffed, the Congregational Association of Massachusetts, and that on grounds of their "unscriptural" government.[77] But relations with these other churches were never on the same intimate basis as those with the German Reformed and Northern and Southern Presbyterians.

A summary of this period in the Dutch Church's history reveals increasing contacts with other churches—through close cooperation and actual union in overseas mission areas, through voluntary associations of its members, through correspondence and exchange of delegates with various denominations, and through plans for cooperation which approached, if they fell short of, union. At the same time that this unitive trend was apparent, a countertrend revealed itself in the three schisms of 1822, 1857, and 1882. The Reformed Church was gradually coming out of her shell, but it was a struggle.

V

Advance and Retreat (1886-1893)

Although the conference between committees of the Dutch and German Reformed Churches held in 1874 to discuss union achieved no positive results, interest in organic union between these two denominations continued at a high level until, in 1886, two Classes overtured the General Synod of the Reformed Church in America to take steps looking toward union. The Classis of Philadelphia, located in a stronghold of the German Church, did not have any concrete proposal of its own to offer, but simply asked in a rather timid way that the General Synod "entertain with kind and careful considera- tion any overtures that may come from the Reformed Church in the United States (German), or from the lower judicatories of our own church, looking towards closer ecclesiastical union."[1] The Classis of Monmouth, in the Synod of New Brunswick (New Jersey), took a bolder approach, and with breadth of vision, resolved

That the General Synod be and hereby is requested to do all in its power to bring together in organized unity the Reformed Churches of the New World, that from the Atlantic to the Pacific, the Continent may be girded with churches upholding the tried and unchangeable doctrines of the Heidelberg Catechism, consolidated as one body and animated by one Spirit.[2]

Both the Dutch and the German Reformed Churches were strug- gling to keep up with both the Westward movement in America and the heavy influx of immigrants, and the Monmouth overture recog- nized that consolidation of the two churches would provide greater strength and efficiency.

The Committee on Overtures of the 1886 General Synod, in con- sidering these two overtures, was certain that any request from the German Church would be carefully considered, and indicated an awareness of strong sentiment in the Dutch Church in favor of such a union. Because the Committee was not sure that organic union would be the best solution, however, they recommended that the President of the General Synod appoint a committee to confer with a similar committee from the German Church, and to bring to the next Synod any information they might obtain, but particularly "to consider carefully the legal bearing of such a union upon our own Church property."³ Such a committee was appointed, with Dr. W. J. R. Taylor, a prominent minister who had served the denomination in several interdenominational activities, as chairman.

Before Dr. Taylor's committee had opportunity to report to the next General Synod, the Particular Synod of Chicago (representing six western classes composed primarily of recent Dutch immigrants) sent in an overture declaring that it was the sense of that Synod that "any agitation of organic union with any other denomination" was "unwise, and detrimental to our church work."⁴ No specific reasons were given for their opposition, nor was it explained how or why church union would be detrimental to that Synod's work.

At the same time the Classes of Albany and Schenectady went off in another direction. They overtured the General Synod to take action looking toward union with the Presbyterian Church in the U. S. A. Faced with these two opposite viewpoints, the Overtures Committee of the 1887 Synod tried to balance them against each other, and found that the six western classes of the Synod of Chicago outweighed the two classes in the Synod of Albany, completely ignoring the attitudes and desires of the classes which had not expressed themselves by overture. The Committee's conclusions, which were adopted by the General Synod, were that present efforts toward church union were not "wise, or hopeful of good to the church," and that, rather than agitate and disrupt the church with vain questions, all ministers and members should do their duty faithfully and loyally until the workings of the Holy Spirit "indicate . . . that our denominational work is done."⁵

At the same session of General Synod (1887), Dr. Taylor's Committee on Union with the Reformed Church in the United States presented its report. They had been unable to meet with a like committee or the German Church, because its triennial Synod had not yet had an opportunity to act upon the question, but they had been gathering information and opinions which they summarized under five main headings: 1) a study of earlier historical relations and efforts for union; 2) a conviction that although the ultimate aim should be organic union, neither church was now ready for it; 3) a unanimous conviction that some sort of closer union should be established; 4) that that closer union could be either conventional and cooperative, or a federal alliance, each retaining autonomy without fusion while working together on benevolent projects; and 5) there ought to be more fellowship, interchange, and acquaintance between the two denominations.[6] Adequate time should be taken to prepare for union, because "a merely sentimental and mechanical union of any kind would be utterly useless."[7] The General Synod, in spite of its agreement with the Overtures Committee that present efforts toward church union were not wise or good, voted to continue the Committee and receive its report.

The General Synod of the Reformed Church in the United States, meeting in Akron, Ohio, in 1887, appointed a committee on union similar to the one already appointed by the Dutch Church, and these two committees met together for a two-day conference in December 1887 at the Marble Collegiate Church in New York City. They organized themselves into a Joint Committee, with Dr. Thomas G. Apple of the German Church as president and Dr. J. A. De Baun of the Dutch Church as secretary. Many opinions and viewpoints were expressed, but the sentiment was unanimously in favor of union. The only differences expressed were in regard to the methods to be used to bring about the union. The Joint Committee finally resolved to hold a popular convention in Philadelphia, at which papers could be read by various persons on different aspects of the union. A sub-committee was also appointed to work out terms of union.[8]

With high hopes and great enthusiasm the general Conference on Union between the Reformed Church in America and the Reformed Church in the United States met in the First (German) Reformed Church of Philadelphia on April 3, 1888, at which "the matured views of leading representatives of both communions upon fundamental topics" were discussed.[9] Delegates were present from nineteen of the thirty-three classes of the Dutch Church, representing all four particular synods, and from seven district synods of the German Church. The eleven major addresses given, and a transcription of the discussions which followed, were published in a brochure which became the study guide for the whole discussion of union in the two denominations.[10] In the introduction to this brochure, the Committee informs its readers that "there was no manifestation of mere sentimental gush, and yet there was genuine enthusiasm, engendered by the remarkable unanimity exhibited in all the papers."[11]

Dr. T. G. Apple, professor of Church History at the Seminary in Lancaster, gave the opening address of the Conference, in which he spoke of the close relations between the two denominations in the past, their common heritage in the Reformation, and their devotion to the Heidelberg Catechism. The present divided state of the church was abnormal, he said, and must be rectified in order to defeat the anti-Christ of infidelity and heathenism. Sacrifice may be demanded, not of principle but of partisan spirit. These two churches should unite on the centralities of the Apostles' Creed and the Heidelberg Catechism, and subordinate other differences.[12]

A Dutch Reformed speaker recalled the suspension of correspondence between the two churches more than thirty years before (at the time of the "Mercersburg theology" controversy), how that breach had pained him, and how pleased he was to see it now being healed. "To the Classis of Amsterdam it seemed to be a fixed conclusion," he said, "that all the Reformed in America, including all Presbyterians, were one, and in the nature of things must be one." In those early colonial days, the Dutch, German and French churches in this country were all in exactly the same relation to the Synods in the Netherlands. He put before the assembly this question: "If the Holland and German churches were once so closely related and combined, when, why and how were they ever separated?"[13]

The Rev. E. T. Corwin, historian of the Dutch Church, discussed the historical and doctrinal relations of the two churches, reminding his audience that both the Dutch and German churches had been constituent parts of the Church of Holland until 1793. It is therefore not a new union which is sought, but a re-establishment of an old union. Allusions were made to the proposed Triennial Convention of the Dutch and German Churches in the 1840's, and its discontinuance because of the "Mercersburg Theology." Mr. Corwin attributed this breach to misconceptions, and in the Peace Conference of 1879, in which the German divisions were settled, he saw the seeds of hope for further successful union.[14]

Speaking on "Unity in Diversity," Professor J. H. Dubbs of Lancaster pointed out that there were differences between the Dutch and German Reformed Churches in Europe, with Hollanders accusing Germans of "flattening out the distinctive doctrines of the church" and Germans declaring that they "could not breathe freely in the keen theological atmosphere of Holland." The Germans were not interested in being bound to the Canons of the Synod of Dort and the Belgic Confession as the Dutch were, although they held these standards in respect. Dubbs quoted Dr. Schaff as saying, "The Reformed confessions are all variations of one theme. The difference is confined to minor details." Therefore, said Dubbs, in the words "of the great Augustine: 'Let there be in necessary things, unity; in doubtful things, liberty; in all things, charity.' "[15] A Dutch Church representative agreed with Dubbs and Schaff in indicating that there is no conflict between the Heidelberg Catechism and the

Canons of the Synod of Dort, the former held by both churches, the latter only by the Dutch Church. In fact, he pointed out, in places the Canons are more liberal in interpretation than is the Catechism.[16]

A statistical comparison showed that the German Church was about twice as large as the Dutch Church. The Dutch Church's main strength was in New York, New Jersey, and Michigan, while the German Church was strong in Pennsylvania, Ohio, and Maryland. Neither the congregations nor the educational institutions overlapped geographically. Both were failing to extend themselves in the West, and this could best be remedied by union.[17]

On April 4, the second day of the Conference, representatives of both denominations spoke about obstacles to union and methods of overcoming them, and then about the advantages of union. Professor William V. V. Mabon of the Theological Seminary in New Brunswick stated that the major obstacles were indifference arising from ignorance and distance from each other, and estrangement of the two churches as a result of their departure from the principal purpose of their organization—the evangelization of the world. He listed frequent objections to union, but denied their validity. Race was no problem, because the Dutch and Germans were both Teutonic, but in any case, the Gospel breaks down the walls of race. Language wasn't a valid objection, because English was becoming the predominant language in both. The only difference in customs was that the German Church emphasized Confirmation, while the Dutch required profession of faith, but it had to be admitted that hasty admission to church membership could occur in both churches. Polity was identical; cultus—liturgy and sacraments—was the same. Property settlements would not be a problem, the lawyers said. No one would be displaced from the church boards, because a larger church would require more secretaries. The German Church did not subscribe to the Canons of the Synod of Dort nor to the Belgic Confession, but this could be solved a) by the German Churches again accepting them as when under the Classis of Amsterdam; or b) by each Synod maintaining its own standards; or c) by adopting an explanatory statement, "denoting the sense in which the three standards are not required to be understood, as expressing the sense of Scripture doctrine."[18] A minister of the German Church agreed with Professor Mabon that although there were slight differences in emphasis, the biggest problems were ignorance and prejudice, whereby misstatements about each other were made.[19]

In regard to the advantages of union, one speaker explained that greater size and influence would bring an end to the question,

"Reformed from what?" Union would add to the efficiency of both churches, eliminating the waste of energy and resources. The two churches would complement each other, because the German Church had greater results in home mission work, the Dutch in foreign missionary work; the Dutch Church was more concerned about creed and catechism, the German about liturgy and worship. Said he, "We have looked into each other's faces and said, 'Why, how much you look like mother, who lived over the sea.'" Union would be a great force for further Christian unity in this country, but, he asked, "How can we preach Christian unity when we who are as near alike as two peas in a pod cannot come together on a common platform of Christian work?"[20] The Rev. Peter Moerdyke, from the Dutch Church in Grand Rapids, listed many advantages to be gained from union: It would give an opportunity for cooperation, inasmuch as dogmatism and sectarian bitterness were passing away; separation required apologies and defensiveness; union would remove the confusion of names of the two churches; it would rectify an historic error; it would perpetuate the Reformed Church in this country, which might otherwise be absorbed into the Presbyterian Church; the German churches in Pennsylvania and Ohio would fill in the geographical gap between the Dutch East and West; it would give ministers a wider choice of field; it would help in conserving for the denomination members who moved elsewhere; it would give classis meetings more weight and power; the educational institutions would benefit from larger enrollments; it would broaden the Dutch Church's concept of home missionary work; and it would be of lasting benefit to a church to be thoroughly aroused and quickened by a new departure.[21]

In the discussion period which followed the presentation of these papers, only one remark was made against union with the German Church, and that was by a non-Dutch minister in the Dutch Church who preferred union with the Presbyterians.[22] The remarkable unanimity of opinion at the Conference led the Committee to look even further into the future, in their preface to the published papers of the Conference:

> We pray that this union, should it be successfully consummated, may be the harbinger of a still more extensive union of the Reformed Churches of this country, and when the 20th century dawns upon us may the time have come when all the Evangelical Churches of America shall be ripe for some form of union that shall best concentrate their energies and activity for the extension and final victory of our blessed Redeemer's Kingdom![23]

The General Synod of the Dutch Church, meeting in 1888, received an overture from the Classis of Wisconsin concerning organic union with the Reformed Church in the United States, "deprecating the agitation of the subject, and uttering a protest against any measures looking to such result."[24] The Overtures Committee refused to consider this protest because no plan had yet been presented by Dr. Taylor's committee on union;[25] rather, the General Synod received a number of recommendations from the committee, which stated that a closer union was desirable, that all should inform themselves more fully on the matter, and that the papers presented at the Philadelphia Conference should be circulated and studied.[26]

The 1889 General Synod received only a progress report, but the thinking of the Committee now was that there was no prospect of immediate organic union, but rather a federal union which would enable the two churches to work together. All the arguments in favor of union were again rehearsed. The Committee evidently was aware of rumblings against union because it cautioned against premature judgment of the question: "Especially do we deprecate the formation of conclusions upon personal prejudices, local circumstances, narrow surroundings and selfish satisfaction with our own ecclesiastical condition."[27]

By the time the 1890 General Synod assembled, the Joint Committee on Union had met, and concluded that the best solution would be a federal union effected by the creation of a new supreme judicatory, the Federal Synod, which would have ultimate authority in all new mission activity at home and abroad, and all new educational work, but which would leave existing institutions under the control of the previous Synods, unless that control was voluntarily given up. The Committee found the logic of this Federal Union in the writings of John Calvin and inherent in the Presbyterian system of government:

> This idea of Federal Union is not original with the illustrious framers of our National Constitution. It dates far back of them to John Calvin . . . It is immanent in the entire Presbyterian organization and movement of the Reformed Churches of Christendom. The Presbytery or Classis is the Federal Union of individual churches. The district or particular synod is the Federal Union of the individual classes or presbyteries. The General Synod or the General Assembly is the Federal Union of the individual Synods. A Federal Union of General Synods or Assemblies would be the natural de-

velopment and highest exponent of the system, and the next grand
upward movement for the unification of hitherto separated, yet
affiliated denominations, like our own.[28]

For the first time the Committee took note of declining membership
and number of churches in the East because of changing population,
and expressed doubt about the long continuance of separate denominational life.[29]

The completed Plan of Union was presented to both Reformed
Churches in 1891 for their consideration. It consisted of a proposed
Constitution with a preamble, thirteen articles, and five recommendations. The articles provided for a new ecclesiastical assembly, to
be called "The Federal Synod of the Reformed Churches," which
was to be composed of sixteen ministers and sixteen elders from
each denomination, to meet annually. To it would be committed
powers relating to Foreign and Domestic Missions; new educational
enterprises; general superintendence of Sunday School interests and
literature, and "other ecclesiastical matters such as shall be determined by concurrent action of both General Synods." Any powers
not specifically delegated to it remained with the General Synods.
It would not interfere with the creed, cultus or government of either
denomination. Amendments might be proposed by either denomination, but must be ratified by both.[30] The recommendations suggested
the union of the missionary and education boards.[31]

The General Synod of the Dutch Church approved the Plan of
Union, thus providing for it to be sent down to the several Classes
for their ratification. The General Synod of the German Church,
meeting at the same time in Philadelphia, unanimously approved
the plan, and in anticipation of its approval by the Classes of the
German Church, appointed its delegates to the first Federal Synod.
Representatives from the German Synod travelled to Asbury Park
to express their joy at the anticipated union to the Dutch Synod.[32]

But as the Classes of the Dutch Church prepared to vote in the
spring of 1892, rumblings of opposition to the plan began to come
out of the West, chiefly from Hope College and the newly-
established Western Theological Seminary (1884) in Holland, Michigan. The official paper of the Dutch Church, *The Christian
Intelligencer,* came out strongly in favor of union, but allowed
both sides to be heard. Dr. N. M. Steffens, president of Western
Seminary, expressed his opposition to union by saying that the
proposed union would be one of labor, but not of faith; that it
would be only a shadow of union, because the creed and cultus

of each church was being left intact; but that real union was impossible because the Heidelberg Catechism was not sufficient as a confession of faith, inasmuch as both Arminians and Calvinists could subscribe to it. "I maintain," he said, "that we represent different types of reformed Christianity. And I, for one, am not prepared to surrender my position to that of the German Reformed Church."[33]

An attack from another direction came when Dr. Herman Berg, son of the Dr. Joseph Berg who left the German Church for the Dutch at the time of the Mercersburg controversy, insisted that the plan did *not* keep intact the autonomy, creed, cultus, and property of the Dutch Church, nor secure proper representation in the government of the united church. Berg claimed that for the Dutch the name Reformed meant "Calvinistic," but for the Germans it meant only "Protestant;" also that the Dutch Church was an American Church, while the other was a German Church. He asked why the churches had separated in 1793, and why they failed to unite in the 1840's, suggesting that doctrinal differences separated them, and that the new union would force the Dutch to subsidize heretical preaching. To settle the question, he quoted Calvin: "Innovations are always dangerous, and often harmful."[34]

A report by the Rev. Henry Straks of Cleveland in the March 2 issue of *The Christian Intelligencer* told of a conference of delegates of both churches, at which Dr. Steffens spoke on the negative side of the question of union. "We cannot allow texts of Scripture, supporting the unity of spirit in general, nor individual opinion or sentiment, to mislead us in this important matter. This question is of a church-political nature. Facts must be considered and weighed. Sentiment cuts no figure here." One of the facts that concerned Dr. Steffens had to do with money. The Dutch Church was considered wealthy, yet Dr. Steffens' new seminary had little, so he quickly informed the Germans not to expect any Dutch money. He criticized them for spending too much money on home missions and not enough on foreign missions. Union with the unenthusiastic Germans would dampen the Dutch Church's zeal for foreign missions: "Pour six gallons of cold water with one gallon of boiling, and what can we expect the temperature to be but cool?"[35]

In yet another article in the church paper, Dr. Steffens argued that the proposed federal union would result in centralization, which was not true Presbyterianism. Yet he admitted that the Churches of the Netherlands, convened in General Synod at Dordrecht in 1618-1619, "formed a federal union, the only kind of organic union known to them."[36]

The editors of *The Christian Intelligencer* wrote frequently in favor of union, and from time to time tried to answer the criticisms of the plan. Other voices joined them. Dr. E. Winter took note of the prominence being given the so-called "race question," but insisted that it should be yielded to higher considerations. "Has a German soul less value than a Dutch soul—or either, less than an American soul?" he asked. He tried to see how the Dutch Church could help the German Church, rather than estimating how it would weaken the Dutch Church.[37] Dr. J. A. De Baun, a member of the Committee on Union, warned that the church should not expect too much of the proposed union, because the immediate results might be disappointing. It would, however, be the beginning of a wider federation with other Reformed and Presbyterian bodies.[38] In reply to Dr. Berg, who questioned whether the Dutch Church received proper representation in the proposed plan, he said:

My greatest surprise is in the objection that the Federal Constitution fails to secure to our church its just and proper representation in the government of the united Church. If this objection had come from the German Church, I think my mouth would have been closed. They outnumber us, in round numbers, three to one. Some of us Dutchmen had an elaborate arrangement to propose, by which we hoped to so arrange representation that we should not be overwhelmed, necessarily, by the force of numbers; but we had the elaborateness all taken out of us, . . . by the spontaneous and unanimous offer of our German brethren to have a representation by equal numbers from the two churches.[39]

But some people didn't want union on any terms, he observed. "In one section of our church there have been ominous mutterings of threatened secession if the union should be effected."[40]

An editorial in the church paper in March explained the "triumphalist" attitude toward church union held by opponents of the present plan: "Christian union is alone attainable by every other Church owning their mistakes and coming over and into the one true Church of Jesus Christ which, of course, is ours. On this basis we fear even a measurable healing of the divisions of Christendom must await the millenium."[41] If the American states had been content to remain divided because of possible difficulties, **there** would have been no nation; yet that is what opponents of federal church union seek to do, the editor concluded.[42]

Dr. J. Elmendorf, a leading minister in the Dutch Church, emphasized that this Church had been given an opportunity to lead the way, first in union with the German Church, and thereafter in a pan-Presbyterian federation.

It would be passing strange and pitiable if our church, having been one of two to lead in the formulation of a plan, should cast away her leadership, just when the church at large is recognising, applauding and accepting the principle and declaring itself ready to join the movement . . . If our favoured Church shall prove that she has not come to the Kingdom for such a time as this . . . , the gracious honour which might have adorned her in the van of the glorious movement toward a real union of the hosts of the Lord, shall rest upon those who were more obedient to his call.[43]

By the end of April, 1892, it looked as though the apprehensions of those favoring union had been unnecessary. Over two-thirds of the Classes and fully nine-tenths of the churches had recorded themselves as favoring the Federal Union.[44] All that remained to be done before the plan would come into effect was the final ratification and declarative act of the General Synod. This was the high-water mark for the Dutch Church. Never before had she gone so far down the road toward church union.

Dr. Taylor, the chairman of the Committee on Union, had died during the year past, so his replacement, Dr. J. A. De Baun, presented the majority report of his committee to the General Synod in June. After reporting the results of the Classes' voting (24 affirmative, 6 officially negative, 3 unofficially reported to have been negative), the committee recommended that the articles of union be adopted, with the understanding that all amendments must be determined by concurrent action of both General Synods, and that the articles were not to be interpreted as conflicting with the denominational constitution. Further, out of consideration for those who had doubts about the plan, the committee recommended an amendment which would allow the General Synods to take back from the Federal Synod any powers delegated to it, with one year's notice. In spite of this modification, the majority report was lost, and a minority report was adopted, providing that action on the question be deferred until the next General Synod, inasmuch as some Classes had had objections to the plan, and as there was also a proposal before General Synod regarding a wider federal union including all Reformed and Presbyterian churches.[45] The vote was 78 to 48 in favor of the minority report. Most of the names in the affirmative list were Western Dutch, but because of the mention of a possible pan-Presbyterian union, those favoring such a union also voted in the affirmative, as well as those favoring union with the German Church but frightened by the West's threat of schism.

The year's delay was regarded by those favoring union as simply a necessary annoyance, during which they hoped the West would come around to the union viewpoint. The editor of *The Christian Intelligencer,* in commenting on the General Synod decision, said

A strong opposition appeared against the measure, composed mainly of the delegates from the churches of Hollanders. They were entitled to be heard. Their opinions are to be regarded with respect. This journal does not agree with them, a fact well known; but their rights are to be freely granted and to be maintained. . . . Our generous and energetic Holland brethren have not had the experience in union Christian efforts which many of us have had during the past forty years . . . They have not been in the rising tide of desire for a larger and more evident union of Christians of every name, as many of us have been. Their life has been more apart, more self-contained. It is for them to consider a conviction we entertain . . . that the foreign element in the United States is retarding, and in some movements has checked American progress on certain moral lines . . . In opposing the federation of American Christian denominations we believe they are standing in the way of the fulfilment of a desire and conviction of American Christians, which is the outgrowth of a God-given experience, and therefore, are hindering what thousands believe to be the progress of American Christianity.[46]

The editor was certain that if the question had come up before a quarter of the delegates of Synod had been excused, or if the issue had been clearly between adoption or rejection of the plan, the majority report would have been passed by a decisive vote.[47]

To those who opposed union with the German Church, however, the year's delay was an opportunity to marshall all their previous arguments against union, present them frequently to the public, and add to them others that came to mind. *The Christian Intelligencer,* the denominational paper, had to print both sides of the argument, but *De Hope,* a Dutch paper published at Hope College in Michigan, could be used by the Western Dutchmen to present only their arguments. By the fall of 1892 the editors of the church

paper were tiring of this advantage the opponents of union had
gained, and openly stated that the opposition sentiment was being
fostered in the columns of *De Hope,* by appealing to well-known
prejudices. When the editors of *De Hope* (including Dr. Steffens
of Western Seminary, who three years later joined the Presbyterian
Church) asked what prejudice was being appealed to, they were
given this answer:

> It is well known that our Holland churches are strongly ortho-
> dox, and because unfamiliar with English religion and theological
> speech, predisposed to be suspicious that what is not expressed in
> Dutch terms has about it more or less of unsoundness. Now the
> fair and right thing for a paper conducted by those who know
> better, addressed to such a constituency, was to disabuse their
> minds of such a prejudice.
> On the contrary, *De Hope* has for a year past teemed with insin-
> uations and suggestions that there is no straight orthodoxy except
> among the Dutch, and has given the impression that even the
> Eastern section of the church is none too sound, and that the Ger-
> man Church is dangerously heretical.[48]

The discussion for and against church union continued in the
denomination and in the pages of the church paper through the
spring of 1893, as long as there was any chance to influence the
voting in the classes. The opponents, in addition to their argument
that no union was thinkable with those who did not accept the
Canons of the Synod of Dort and the Belgic Confession, criticized
the German Church for its shortage of ministers, its lower level
of financial contributions to benevolence, its smaller role in foreign
missions.[49] They also argued that the German Church was not
sufficiently centralized,[50] although earlier their fears had been
that the new church would be too centralized for their comfort.
One elder urged that the church "go slow," but gave no reason
except that he felt union should take place only when 100% of
the church was in favor of it.[51] Toward the end of the debate, a
Western Seminary professor raised Warfield's criticism of Professor E. V. Gerhart's book, "The Institution of the Christian Religion." Warfield had charged the Lancaster professor with heresy,
and this was repeated with glee by union opponents.[52] The chief
argument, however, which was raised again and again, was that
union would result in schism.[53] That this was no idle threat was
clear from the schism which had occurred in the West just ten
years previous, when the General Synod refused to take a stand

against Freemasonry. Some of the Eastern ministers who were originally in favor of the union changed their positions because of the threat of schism.[54]

An "Observer," writing in *The Christian Intelligencer,* in reply to the West's threat of secession, accurately described their attitude:

> He [Dr. H. E. Dosker of Western Seminary] intimates that the people of the West who object to Federal Union are most loyal to our church; so loyal that they fear nothing so much as that the church shall prove disloyal to herself. Now I submit that this is the plea of the professional seceder. *He* is always loyal; the church in general is *disloyal*; ergo, out he goes![55]

Dr. Talbot W. Chambers, minister of the Collegiate Church, and himself very conservative theologically, felt that the West's bluff should be called:

> The only serious objection is . . . that they would secede. So important is the principle of federation that is at stake that the risk must be run. If our brethren shut their eyes to the advantages of the scheme, and look only at some possible ill results, and therefore are unwilling to submit to the voice of the majority, we will be very sorry and exceedingly regret their departure, but we cannot for their sakes violate our sense of duty, and abandon a measure which seems to us of inestimable importance to the general interest of the Reformed all over the world . . . Calvin said he was willing to cross ten oceans if he could heal the divisions of Protestantism. Surely we should be willing to cross a narrow brook if we can heal a single division among the Reformed.[56]

The editor of *The Christian Intelligencer* rightly foresaw what would happen to the Dutch Church if the majority favoring union yielded to the minority opposed to it:

> If Federal Union is defeated, it will be purely and simply because once again a sentiment has been worked up until claimed to be beyond the control of its originators, and the argument is made that the church must bow before it or a fearful disruption will take place. In 1880 it was freemasonry, now it is the danger of heterodoxy. In both cases a pretext is used to compass the end, and when the mischief is wrought, we are coolly informed, "No one is master of the situation," and if the church does not acquiesce a serious secession is inevitable . . . Had not the General Synod better retire into "innocuous desuetude" and let the policy of the church be directed by a committee in Holland, Michigan?[57]

The General Synod of 1893 was informed that all classes had reported their final reactions to the Plan of Union, and that of the 34 Classes, sixteen had voted in the affirmative, and eighteen in the negative. Of those voting affirmatively, only two were Western Classes, but they were English-speaking of old American stock. Of those voting negatively, seven were Western Dutch classes. The reason that some of the Eastern classes voted negatively was indicated by the reason the Classis of South Long Island gave for its disapproval:

Whereas the idea of Federal Union has, in the providence of God taken the larger form of the Federation of the Churches of the Reformation, therefore Resolved, that the South Classis of Long Island overture the General Synod to invite the cooperation of the German Reformed Church in perfecting that plan of Federal Union that shall include all the Reformed Churches holding the Presbyterian system.[58]

The General Synod accepted the Committee's report recommending that, inasmuch as the Classes defeated the Plan of Union, further consideration be indefinitely postponed.[59]

And so the Dutch Reformed Church lost its best opportunity for church union. Federal union was not the same as organic union, to be sure; it was a new experiment. But by uniting the missionary and educational work of the two churches, the federal union would undoubtedly have evolved into an organic union. The plan was not perfect, but it would have been an interesting and workable experiment. The majority of the Dutch Church members and classes favored it, but they yielded to the minority who threatened secession. Never before in their history had they been so far along the road to union. And never again in their history to the present have they had the opportunity to approach church union so closely, because in the years since the 1890's, the Western Dutch wing of the church has grown steadily larger until now it is almost equal in size to the older, ecumenical-minded Eastern branch of the church.

VI

New Efforts to Federate and Unite (1893-1930)

Federations & Councils

Church federation was a popular idea at the turn of the twentieth century, both in the Reformed Church and in Protestantism in general. It seemed to many the best way to manifest the unity of Christ's Church. Part of its appeal lay in the fact that a number of groups could be brought under one umbrella without sacrificing much of any group's freedom, power or peculiarity. The federal union attempted by the Reformed churches, Dutch and German, in the previous period was more than the Dutch were ready for. Because of and in spite of that defeat, new schemes of federation now came before the General Synod. These federation efforts of the first third of the twentieth century will be described first, and they will be followed by an exploration of attempts at organic union.

One of the proposals for federation, coming from the Presbyterian Church in the U. S. A. before the federal union scheme had been acted upon, may have helped defeat the federal union. For many Reformed Church ministers, association with the Presbyterian Church seemed more natural than with the German Reformed. The Presbyterian proposal of 1890, received the next year by the General Synod, visualized something similar to the Evangelical Alliance, with the following significant differences: it would be composed of denominations rather than individuals, and it would have certain powers assigned to it. These powers would be in the realm of united work in city and rural areas, in comity arrangements across the nation, and in a united voice in lobbying and propaganda. Only the Reformed-Presbyterian group of churches was initially invited.[1] The Reformed Church accepted the invitation, and in 1893 a preliminary plan was approved for a "Federal Council" of Reformed Churches.[2] It took effect in 1895 after the Classes and the General Synod had acted favorably upon it. The title of the new organization was "The Federal Council of the

Reformed Churches in the United States of America, holding the
Presbyterian System."[3] Cooperation in home and foreign missionary
work was to be promoted, the influence of Protestant Christianity
upon the nation was to be strengthened, and correspondence with
other bodies maintained. But there was to be no interference with
creed, worship, government or discipline of the member churches.
Joined with the Dutch Reformed in this venture were the Associate Reformed Synod of the South, the Cumberland Presbyterian
Church, the German Reformed Church, the Reformed Presbyterian Church, the United Presbyterian Church, and the Presbyterian
Church, U. S. A.[4]

The weakness of federation is revealed in the fact that once
this Federal Council was established, nothing further was heard
about it. It seems not only to have disappeared, but to have been
forgotten, for no mention is ever made of it again. But when in
1902 the Reformed Presbyterian Church proposed that the "important matter of closer cooperation or unity of organization
among the Presbyterian Churches of the United States" be discussed, some of the same men were appointed to the committee
who set up the earlier Federal Council![5] And after discussing the
problem for three years with the same churches previously involved, they again adopted the title of "The Federal Council
of the Reformed Churches in the United States of America, holding the Presbyterian System."[6] The aims and limitations were
essentially the same as before. Both of these plans differed from
the earlier "Federal Union" with the German Reformed, in that
they did not provide for a united synod to govern the member
churches. In both cases, the Federal Councils did not require
consolidation of churches, but only cooperation between churches
without loss of identity.[7] When the plan of federation was finally
adopted in 1906, it was called "Articles of Agreement," and the
proposed "Federal Council" had become simply the "Council."
The Cumberland Presbyterian Church dropped out of the Council,
and the (Southern) Presbyterian Church in the U. S. joined.[8] In
1911 it was voted to combine home mission work, particularly
among the Negroes, of the member denominations of the Council,
and to encourage closer cooperation in education and publications.
In response to proposals that the Council should be amalgamated
with the Alliance of Reformed Churches throughout the World
holding the Presbyterian System, the chairman had this to say:

The work of the [world] Alliance has reference to the Reformed
Churches throughout the world, and is only advisory in its char-

acter. The Council of the Reformed Churches in the United States is composed of delegates directly chosen by our own judicatories, deals only with our national problems, and under the direction of the judicatories, has certain administrative powers as may be seen from the opening section of this report. The confusion of mind on the part of the 'uninitiated,' due to the similarity of names, will be removed by time . . . The possibility of economy in consolidation is very small indeed . . .[9]

In 1913 the Presbyterian Church hoped that the Council could be used to move the denominations onward from federation to actual union.[10] The Reformed Church buried the suggestion in a committee, but it rose again in a 1918 communication. The Synod was more concerned with the revision of the Constitution of the Federal Council. If adopted, this revision would have made the newly-named "General Council" a federal union rather than a federation by uniting certain boards and agencies of the denominations. But unfortunately the pertinent section of the revision was not approved.[11]

The distinction between the Alliance of Reformed Churches holding the Presbyterian System and the General Council (formerly Federal Council, then Council) of Reformed Churches holding the Presbyterian System which had been hoped for in 1911 never became clear or real. The General Council did not, as many hoped, lead to organic union. Finally, in 1927, a step was taken which must have seemed obvious for a long time—the General Council was absorbed into the Western Section of the Alliance of Reformed Churches. It was believed that the limited administrative powers of the General Council would now become part of the Alliance structure, but this did not in fact happen.[12] The Reformed Church today continues as an active member of the World Alliance and its North American Area Council.

Far more fruitful than this pan-Presbyterian attempt at church federation was America's great ecumenical contribution of this period, the Federal Council of Churches. The Social Gospel, and recognition of the need for a united Protestant voice in facing the problems of an industrialized mass society, were major factors in bringing the churches together into this action-oriented, rather than theology-oriented, federation.[13] When asked by the "National Federation of Churches and Christian Workers" for delegates to set up the cooperative body, General Synod did so because it was "in hearty sympathy with the aims and plans of the National Federation."[14] The Inter-Church Conference on Federation met at Carnegie

Hall in November, 1905, and adopted a plan for a Federal Council. The Reformed Church General Synod approved the plan in 1906, and named ten delegates.[15] Thirty-three denominations sent delegates to the opening session in December, 1908, in Philadelphia. A Reformed Church delegate, the Rev. James I. Vance, was elected a vice-president. Since its inception, the Federal Council of Churches of Christ in America, and its successor, the National Council of Churches, have had among its faithful members the Reformed Church in America.

The only other broad cooperative movement among Protestant churches which received attention from the Reformed Church during this period was the ill-starred Interchurch World Movement immediately after World War I. To accomplish great things and fulfill great new purposes this movement hoped to attract a great deal of non-church money. The Synod of 1919 gave tentative approval to cooperation with the movement by its program boards "in so far as they can do so in harmony with their own work."[16] By 1920 it was already obvious that the Interchurch World Movement was a colossal failure.

The attempt of the Interchurch World Movement to secure the cooperation of those who are not active members of Christian Communions has clearly demonstrated that the Church alone has any vital sense of obligation to a sinful and suffering world. The "Friendly Citizen" is a negligible quantity. It may be fairly said that he does not exist. The burden of the world's redemption rests still, where Jesus Christ placed it, on the hearts and shoulders of those who confess him as Master and Lord.[17]

Receipts from "friendly citizens" amounted to about $3 million by 1920, but the Movement's bill to the denominations was over $9 million, and each denomination had to locate new revenue to try to pay its share.[18] The losses on this venture were never recouped.

Union: Reformed Churches

Federation was certainly the main theme of this period, and even federation often proved difficult to achieve, or if easy to achieve then of little value. The editor of the *Christian Intelligencer*, writing soon after the defeat of the plan for union of the two Reformed Churches, questioned "the sincerity of much professed zeal in the cause" of church union,[19] and felt that "the divisive forces are yet stronger in the Churches than the unifying ones; and the present time does not seem propitious for any form of Church Union."[20] In spite of widespread pessimism about the possibilities of church union, proposals for such union kept coming from various quarters and continued to be considered by the denomination. Sometimes, as when the request or interest came from the seceded Christian Reformed Church, the proposal would be dismissed with slightly-disguised disdain.[21] The negative attitude arose because the Christian Reformed Church began its proposal with questions about the Reformed Church's position on Freemasonry and her fidelity to the doctrinal standards. The Reformed Church reacted negatively to the Christian Reformed Church's proposal for "mutual attention that no one depart in doctrine, liturgy or discipline from Reformed principles." At other times proposals would receive more serious concern. In 1903 the Presbyterian Church in the United States, having received seven overtures from presbyteries and synods to that end, stated its desire to appoint a Committee of Conference to meet with a similar committee from the Reformed Church, "to consider the whole question of closer relations and a possible organic union of these two churches."[22] The Reformed Church was willing to appoint such similar committee, but apparently the matter was lost in confusion and enthusiasm about pan-Presbyterian federation, in which the Presbyterian Church, U.S., was not initially interested.[23]

Twenty years after the defeat of the plan of union between the Dutch and German Reformed Churches, the Classis of New Brunswick in 1913 overtured General Synod to try once again to effect a closer relation between the two sister churches. A committee was appointed to meet with the German Reformed, whose response was enthusiastic, especially if this were to lead to organic union.[24] The Dutch Reformed committee, being composed of that Church's delegates to the General Council of Reformed Churches, seems to have thought more in terms of federation, so that in 1917 the German Reformed suggested that for federative purposes, the General Council of Reformed Churches was all that was necessary.[25] The question was re-opened by several overtures from Classes of the Dutch Reformed Church in 1925 and 1926, asking for federal or organic union with the German Church. The German Church that year, like the Dutch, appointed a committee to discuss the question. In the 1927 report to General Synod Dr. T. H. Mackenzie, chairman (and ex-Presbyterian), said,

Short of organic union there is little that could be accomplished by a conference of the Committees of the two denominations and as the General Synod of 1925 explicitly instructed your Committee to exclude the idea of organic union from negotiations we have not thought it wise to move further in this matter. . . . It would be neither courteous to other churches nor dignified for our own body to negotiate on the question of an organic union so long as we have no reasonable assurance that Organic Union is desired by our Church.[26]

If the 1925 Synod did indeed give explicit instructions to exclude the idea of organic union from these negotiations, it must have given them privately to Dr. Mackenzie, as there is no evidence of such instructions in the Minutes. Mackenzie may well have been accurate, however, in his assessment of the mood of the denomination in regard to organic union. In any case, in this fashion the last opportunity to unite the Dutch and German branches into one strong Reformed church disappeared.

Union: Presbyterian Churches

The other denominations which continued to fascinate the Reformed Church were the Presbyterian Church U. S., and the Presbyterian Church in the U. S. A. For many ministers and members, these churches rather than the German Reformed were the ones most familiar and similar to the Dutch Reformed. The first major encounter with the Presbyterian Church in this period was an unusual instance of union by dissolution. The Reformed Church had begun mission work among the Oklahoma Indians in 1895, and in 1900 began work among white settlers also. By 1906 a number of churches had been established, and a classis was organized.[27] Great enthusiasm for the work continued for a few years, but by 1911 the Reformed Church was ready to give up. Officially, the Mission Board said only that "continued occupation of the field by the Reformed Church would be an unwarranted sacrifice of men and money."[28] Hence the churches should be transferred to another denomination. The decision was made to transfer some of them to the Southern Presbyterian Church and others to the Presbyterian Church in the U. S. A. Dr. W. H. S. Demarest, one-time president of Rutgers and later president of New Brunswick Seminary, attributed the Reformed Church's failure to the fact that "those people out there had no background in the Dutch Reformed tradition."[29]

A new interest in schemes of Presbyterian union arose after the end of World War I. In 1918 the Presbyterian Church invited the

Reformed and other churches to send delegates to consider "the subject of an organic union of all evangelical churches."[30] The Reformed Church indicated that it considered such a proposal too broad, as indicated also by its refusal that year to allow formal discussion of a local union of Reformed, Presbyterian and Episcopal congregations in the city of New Brunswick.[31] In 1919 the Reformed Church declared its belief that concern for general evangelical unity should be expressed through the Federal Council of Churches,[32] and also indicated interest in union with the Presbyterians.[33] Thus in 1920 a "Plan of Union" was prepared and presented to the General Synod, as well as to the Presbyterian General Assemblies. While not strictly a plan of organic union, it was more than a "federal council" type of unity. A representative united assembly of the joining churches was to be given power to receive other churches; superintend home and foreign missions, publication, pensions, evangelism and stewardship; exercise judicial functions and settle comity questions; and to meet biennially.[34]

The General Synod of 1920 endorsed the tentative Plan of Union, and appointed a representative committee to help draft a Constitution.[35] It also re-affirmed its interest in a proposal to create a central board to administer Presbyterian and Reformed foreign missions, made to the previous General Synod.[36] The 1921 Synod received the proposed Constitution of "The Presbyterian Reformed Churches in America," with the committee's recommendation that it be adopted. It incorporated all of the concepts and powers of the tentative plan of union. But before the Synod could vote on the plan, the Presbyterian bodies had already defeated it. Dr. J. Boyd Hunter, editor of the Reformed Church's *Christian Intelligencer*, suggested that "the experiences of our Presbyterian brethren in the Interchurch World Movement seem to have set back for some time the fervor of their zeal for unity."[37] The committee members present at Synod in 1921 issued a supplementary report, in the light of the plan's defeat by sister churches, recommending "that the whole matter be laid on the table indefinitely,"[38] which (because the report was adopted) is where it remains to this day.

In 1928 the Reformed Church in America observed the Tercentenary of the denomination's founding in Nieuw Amsterdam, now New York. The celebration apparently produced a sense of euphoria in some, a sense of frustration and lack of progress in others. Six classes and the Particular Synod of New Brunswick overtured for union with the Reformed Church in the United States, but the committee on Overtures and Judicial Business, under a conservative

chairman, Dr. E. J. Blekkink of Western Seminary, recommended
no action on these grounds:

> External union compared with spiritual union is insignificant. We
> have the spiritual union now to a degree that it was found in the
> Apostolic Church. We believe that these two denominations will do
> better work side by side, in holy zeal for the coming of the Kingdom
> and the glory of the King, both at home and on the foreign field, and
> other lines of work. *Co-operation,* not organic union, must be the
> watch word for some time to come.[39]

The "no action" proposal was lost! Instead a resolution was adopted, calling for a special fact-finding commission "to diligently study
the possibilities of Christian Union," and the program committee
was instructed to provide time "for full and free discussion" at the
1929 Synod.[40]

During the ensuing year the Fact-Finding Commission industri-
ously prepared a five-chapter booklet of over fifty pages, in which it
presented a) advantages and disadvantages of union for the Reformed Church; b) a brief survey of church movements in general;
c) a sketchy history of past relations with the German Reformed
Church and the Presbyterian Church, U. S. A.; and d) conclusions.
Advantages were placed over against disadvantages of union, as it
was argued that the family spirit would not be lost; the per capita
giving would not decline; theologically and liturgically the Reformed Church was at one with other Presbyterians; the courts
would protect property rights; one's heritage would not be lost, but
would be added to; and that John 17 must be interpreted as imply-
ing organic as well as spiritual union.[41] In addition home and foreign
missions would gain, overhead would be cut down, a new name
would be better known than "Reformed," and, the committee believed, church union was the will of God. The section on church
union movements attempted to show that this is the trend of the
times. In pointing out previous relations between the Dutch and
German churches, the numerous and repeated attempts were noted,
but the fact that the German Church was currently negotiating
with the Evangelical Synod (having "Lutheran" elements) and the
United Brethren in Christ (having "Arminian" tendencies) seemed
to the committee sufficient reason to eliminate the German Church
from further consideration.[42]

The review of relations with the Presbyterian Church in the
U. S. A. showed that that church had also frequently shared in

union attempts with the Dutch Church. She had adopted the Heidelberg Catechism of the Dutch as the Dutch had the Westminster Catechism of the Presbyterians. The Presbyterian committee on relations with other churches was unanimously in favor of union with the Dutch Reformed, and the Fact-Finding Commission similarly favored the Presbyterians. The committee urged further fact-finding, an enlarged committee, and no action without "substantial unanimity of all sections of our Church."[43]

Enthusiasm ran high at the 1929 Synod when the Fact-Finding Report was presented. In connection with it Dr. Robert E. Speer of the Presbyterian Church spoke for union, and "it was one of the wonderful efforts of eloquence that come very rarely to the experience of most men, and will be always remembered by those who listened to it."[44] Dr. Daniel Poling, president of Synod, was also eloquent in favor of union. Dr. A. L. Warnshuis and Dr. Albertus Pieters, former missionaries, spoke for union and urged adoption of the report. When the question was put, there was but one vote in the negative.[45]

That negative vote was, no doubt, that of Dr. William Leverich Brower, senior elder of the Collegiate Church, president of the denominational Board of Direction, leader in the Holland Society of New York, an executive of a New York liquor-importing firm, and an eccentric bachelor. Brower received permission to read a paper to the Synod opposing adoption of the report, which he later published under the slightly-disguised pseudonym of "A Veteran Observer."[46] He did not find the "facts" convincing, and felt the committee had been caught up in religious imperialism. Rather than join the Presbyterians, he would prefer the Unitas Fratrum or the Protestant Episcopal Church.[47] He would not be attracted to the Methodists, "where it was enacted that if its ministers smoked their licences would be withdrawn. Their next step in such fanaticism, I presume, would be to advocate the shooting of those of its ministers who persisted in smoking."[48] But all of these choices were unnecessary for him because "if all else were to be swept away by the wreck of the denomination, the Collegiate Church would still survive and with its eleven places of worship has in it the basis of a denomination."[49] He regarded the Reformed Church as an asylum:

To her ranks those who are heartily sick of doctrinal and other disturbances in their denominations can repair, and find peace and satisfaction in her beautiful standards of Faith, whose standards ring true to the Oracles . . . Witness the bitter divisions in the recent assembly of the Presbyterian Church. Do we, my brethren, wish to involve our seminaries in any such questions? . . . An elect lady of recent times, born in a Methodist family . . . exclaimed to me, "By coming into the Reformed Church I have been elevated to a higher spiritual world."[50]

During the course of the year Dr. Brower issued another pamphlet attacking organic union, in which he re-published articles written by others against union. He quoted from the address made by Dr. David J. Burrell on the twenty-fifth anniversary of his pastorate at the Marble Collegiate Church:

> It is vain to rail against the divisions of the church. "Fences make good neighbors." God made men to segregate, like sheep; and segregate they will. "Birds of a feather flock together."[51]

Brower went on to mention Reformed churches in Ceylon, Java, China, Formosa, Japan, Moscow, St. Petersburg, and Constantinople, then stated:

> All these churches were the daughters of the Mother in Holland and many of them remain to this day. Into this family our Reformed Church in America was born, and we must regard our Church as something other than a denomination. We must think of her, to use the words of the beloved Dr. E. J. Blekkink [president of Western Seminary in Michigan], as a *parish* of the Reformed Church. . . . She wishes to remain in her family and retain her family name.[52]

But Brower's biggest attack on union was written by Dr. Albertus Pieters, son of one of the founding fathers of the Michigan Dutch colony, long-time missionary in Japan and later professor at Western Seminary, beloved and revered throughout the West. He had spoken at General Synod in favor of adoption of the Fact-Finding Commission's report, but soon after wrote an article, "The Question of Church Union," in which he stated that the Dutch Reformed would become Presbyterians in spite of tactful attempts to "veil the fact that one body has swallowed up the other."[53] While this might not be a bad thing, because one should not be motivated by sentimental feelings for the past, the drive for union was posited upon the assumption that general organic union was the end goal, and that was to argue against the Reformation. Emphasis should be on spiritual unity rather than organization, he said. "Next to the Roman Catholic Church, it is the Church of England that lays most stress on the necessity for the 'reunion' of Christendom—yet High Church and Low Church live together like cats and dogs, and carry their quarrels even to the House of Commons."[54]

General organic union was undesirable, Pieters claimed, because it would be impossible to preserve both purity of doctrine and religious liberty; to maintain separation of church and state; to preserve democracy in religion. And "such a church would be too large and too influential a body to conduct missionary work abroad without incurring suspicion from foreign governments."[55] Union with the Presbyterians might be a step in the direction of such a general union. "Why should we join the Presbyterians? The 'status quo' has the right of way. The burden of proof lies upon the affirmative."[56]

The voice of the affirmative was to be heard in the land, but mostly from the East. The Classis of Westchester called church union a matter of urgent importance, and the clerk of that Classis wrote in *The Christian Intelligencer*:

We already have churches which may not unfairly be called Reformed in name only, and their number is increasing. Indeed, the time is not far distant when these churches will want to know why they should not affiliate with more powerful denominations with more challenging programs than the Reformed Church can ever present. The alternative to Church Union may well be the secession of some of the most important congregations of our faith.[57]

One young pastor, a scion of one of the most ancient Dutch families in New York, gave six reasons for church union in a series of articles in the church paper: a) the denomination cannot hold a settled constituency because it is located in an area of high transiency; b) the Dutch tradition is no longer an asset in large areas of the church; c) the foreign mission is hindered, rather than aided, by separation; d) union is necessary if America is to be evangelized; e) because of decentralized Presbyterian government, the Dutch would not be swallowed up; f) the best way to honor the pioneering spirit of the early Dutch settlers is similarly to pioneer in finding solutions for our day. "The Holland Society and kindred organizations are better fitted than we to honor and perpetuate the traditions of the Dutch pioneers. The Church of Jesus Christ has more pressing business. Will our children honor us as pioneers, or will they try to forgive our short-sightedness?"[58]

When attacks were made upon the Fact-Finding Commission as a group of "scheming young enthusiasts," it was pointed out that thirty-three leaders of the church were on the commission, including five ex-presidents of General Synod and theological professors. The writer said he did not exaggerate the importance of union as though the Kingdom depended on it, but, he said, "we do justly resent and deprecate prejudiced unwillingness to give any audience to what we may have to say. . . . Such a policy might eventually put the Reformed Church in a position where our children and grandchildren would deplore their parents' woeful lack of foresight."[59]

One of the few proponents of union with the Presbyterians in the western section of the church was Dr. J. E. Kuizenga, a professor at the Western Seminary. In an article in the western church paper, *The Leader,* he mentioned that 45% of the ministers in the East had belonged to another denomination, 29% of them Presbyterian; while in the West 23% had belonged to another denomination, and only 8% Presbyterian. He claimed that many of the older ministers were neutral, most of the younger men enthusiastically favored union, but that some young men were also opposed.[60] Two months later, however, he wrote:

The most serious argument against the proposed merger, it seems to us, is the fact that our Church is not ready for it. Whatever differences there may be among us as to the weight of other reasons, we can all agree of this fact, that more effort to work for Union at this time will be disastrous. It will not be possible to unite, without precipitating new divisions, new secessions; and so we shall make worse the very thing some are so anxious to cure.[61]

And two weeks later, the *Christian Intelligencer* announced Dr. Kuizenga's transfer to Princeton Seminary and the Presbyterian Church. The editor facetiously remarked on the transfer:

With Dr. Kuizenga, Dr. S. M. Zwemer and Dr. John T. Raven now on the faculty of Princeton Seminary it will need only a few other transfers to completely Reform the faculty,—and maybe that is the way Union will win out. Perhaps our friend had this in mind in writing the Leader article, when he advises General Synod to discourage any further talk of Union.[62]

Whatever Kuizenga's motives were in writing his article, he seems accurately to have sensed the mood of the denomination. The Committee on Closer Relations with Other Denominations, appointed at the 1929 General Synod, reported to the 1930 Synod "that it is the sentiment of this Committee that union between the Reformed Church in America and the Presbyterian Church in the United States of America is desirable, provided substantial unanimity of all sections of our Church can be secured."[63] That such substantial unanimity did not exist was made clear to the Committee by regional conferences which had been held throughout the denomination during the year. "Judging from Conferences held in the Particular Synods of New York, New Brunswick, and Albany," the committee reported, "the opinion of the great majority in the East is that the Reformed Church in America could do more effective work for the Kingdom if allied with a denomination having a national appeal. The sectional appeal is no longer vital."[64] But the two western Synods were of the opposite opinion:

Judging from Conferences held in the Particular Synods of Chicago and Iowa, the opinion of the majority in the West is that the Reformed Church in America, as it is, has a distinctive contribution to make to the Kingdom.[65]

The Committee was continued for several more years, but the hope of union died with this reported division of opinion.

This difference of opinion reflected the different sociological situations of the two branches of the church. The eastern churches were located primarily in urban pluralistic settings where not only the Reformed Church, but Protestantism in general, formed a small minority of the total population. In such a setting differences between most Protestant churches seemed insignificant. On the other hand, most western churches were located in rural areas, in Dutch towns or in Dutch ghettoes of larger cities. In their narrowly-defined world the Reformed Church was the dominant, or at least a prominent, force, and total isolation from other Protestant denominations was not uncommon.

The Worcester Affair

An event which had occurred in the church a few years earlier illustrates both the sociological differences, and a difference in approach to theological questions. New Brunswick Theological Seminary proposed in 1923 to hire as professor of theology Dr. Edward Strong Worcester, a Congregational pastor whose father had been a professor at Union Seminary in New York and whose grandfather had been the first secretary of the American Board of

Commissioners for Foreign Missions. Dr. W. H. S. Demarest, president of the Seminary, strongly recommended Worcester's election in his nominating speech at the General Synod, speaking of his soundness on the great essentials of the faith. On minor points, however, Demarest said, Worcester

plainly felt that if he were called and if he were free to consider acceptance, he could sign the professor's formula if understood as accepting the body of Scriptural and gospel doctrine contained in the standards, not as subscribing to every single item or expression in them. Any other understanding than this could hardly be asked or expected of any professor whether from without or from within the church in this day, hundreds of years after those documents were written.[66]

Worcester stated quite plainly where his reservations lay in regard to the Doctrinal Standards. He felt that there was too much emphasis on Adam, and called the doctrine of Adam's federal responsibility for human sin "a bit of the fanciful or allegorizing theology of the rabbinic period in Judaism and similar schools in Christianity, which is worse than meaningless today."[67] He would strike out the word "decrees" and speak instead of God's steadfast purposes, he would soften some extreme words like "accursed idolatry" as a description of the Mass. He, like almost all other ministers, would reject Article 36 of the Belgic Confession, which calls upon the state to enforce theological orthodoxy.[68]

Demarest, and most other ministers in the eastern section of the Reformed Church, might consider these reservations as being within the range of freedom of interpretation. But four Western (or Western Seminary-educated) members of the New Brunswick Board of Superintendents sent copies of Worcester's objections to all members of the General Synod of 1923, "in order that you may act intelligently as you feel the will of God to be, for the glory of His Name and the maintenance of the faith once delivered to the saints."[69] One Western pastor wrote to the Stated Clerk of General Synod:

That N. Brunswick nomination is itself rank heresy. To choose such a man would *disrupt the ch* as sure as Calvinism lives here— The Synod, or thro. com:—should withdraw that name and not permit a discussion to start that will be published far and wide to the shame and horror of the church and to the joy of all the 'liberals' in the land.

That man says he can't sign the formula: the Constitution says—
'you must.' Hence he 1) should, without an-word, have said
no. and 2) Synod has no right to consider his name. If *N.Brswk.*
will stand *for that*, then we do not any longer need N. Br.
Seminary. We can't amend and trim and scale down our standards
for any man. Let us be loyal. [sic][70]

The newspapers, as predicted, had a field day with the fight at
General Synod. The day after the battle opened, one newspaper
began its article by saying, "The General Synod of the Reformed
Church in America was in an uproar at noon today . . ."[71] The
following day, under the heading "Seminary Man Picked After
Fight," it had this to say:

Rev. Edward Strong Worcester of Bellows Falls, Vt., was elected
to the chair of Systematic Theology at the New Brunswick Seminary
by the General Synod of the Reformed Church in America on the
eighth ballot at a secret session concluded here just before midnight,
it was announced today. . . . The vote, which was 147 to forty, broke
a deadlock on the question which had existed since last Saturday,
when the installing of the chair was proposed. Rev. Worcester was
elected on the first ballot cast last night, but the eighth of the convention. The main objection to Dr. Worcester was the fact that he
is a congregationalist and is reported to hold unorthodox views.[72]

A few weeks later, Dr. Demarest received the following information
from one of the members of his Board of Superintendents:

The immediate occasion of this letter is an item in the account
of the Intelligencer of Synod's proceedings; viz. that owing to one
man the unanimity of Dr. Worcester's election was defeated. Now,
that does not sound very gracious, and . . . I was that man. . . .
We were not there indirectly to revise the Creed, so that Dr.
Worcester's beliefs could be made to pass muster. . . . Whether these
Standards express the beliefs of those present at Synod,—that was
not the question at issue. . . . We read much of Modernism these
days. It is all around us. We feared it might have appeared in our
own midst, but thought not. But now Dr. Worcester's views, though
interpreted ever so leniently, gives every promise of furnishing the
seed plot from which the evil crop can spring up. . . . What right
have we to be called a Reformed Church anyway if its principles are
denied? We may in that case as well amalgamate at once with anything in sight. . . . We were within our own house standing guard
over its own peculiar treasures. But our own house was invaded: an
alien economy was there to be set up, and the owners to keep still.
You were a party to this![73]

To another New Brunswick professor the same man indicated that he would never urge another person to attend New Brunswick Seminary, and concluded, "Please do not ask me to save your Modernist program."[74] From that day to the present, the charge is still raised in certain Western circles of the Reformed Church that New Brunswick Seminary is "liberal" or "modernist," and that the eastern section of the church is theologically unreliable.

Progress in Overseas Union

In the face of the strong opposition among the conservative Dutch elements of the Reformed Church to any kind of church union, it is interesting to observe that the overseas mission work of the Reformed Church was included in ever-widening circles of organic union. This policy of overseas union was clearly set forth in an extensive document prepared by the Board of Foreign Missions as early as 1886. It urged full cooperation and comity on the field, both to avoid rivalry and competition, and to reap the advantage of united colleges and theological schools. One united native church in each country was the goal, and to that end unions had already been accomplished in China and Japan, and approval of union given for India. Native financial support and independence were to be achieved as quickly as possible, and the relation to home churches should be voluntary. Missionaries should decide in cooperation with the native churches whether they should belong to the native or to the home church.[75]

In 1901 plans for union in India moved forward, when a plan for a united church was approved, combining the work of the Church of Scotland, the Free Church of Scotland, and the Reformed Church. This had been at Reformed Church initiative, and the General Synod readily approved the plan.[76] The following year the Classis of Arcot, which until then had been a part of the Reformed Church, was transferred to the Synod of South India, because "the native church of India calls for an indigenous church, which shall root deeply in its native soil. The people of India should not be allowed to labor under the impression that it is an exotic."[77] In July 1907 a further scheme of union was adopted, which combined the Synod of South India with the Congregational churches there, resulting in the South India United Church.[78] In 1919 approval was given at the Tranquebar Conference to work toward total Protestant Christian union, including the Anglicans, a movement which was later to culminate in the Church of South India.[79]

At the same time a wider union was developing in China. Very early in the history of the Reformed Church's work in China, that work was combined with English Presbyterian efforts. Now, after World War I, the next logical step was taken to include the Congregational churches in the same united Christian Church. This union, in 1919, meant that all Protestant work in the Amoy (South Fukien) region of China was united in one body.[80] Similar tendencies were occurring in Japan, which however did not have positive results until later.

Why was the Reformed Church able to be a leader in union efforts overseas during this period, while remaining isolationist at home? The answer must be found, in large part, in the fact that the crucial decisions for cooperation and union overseas were made very early, before the western section of the church, with its belief in the distinctive witness of the *Dutch* Reformed, gained too much power.[81] Once the decisions had been made to work for an indigenous Reformed-Presbyterian church in each country, the movement toward further unions had a momentum all its own. In addition, of course, there are the general factors facing all overseas work which tend toward united efforts: few Christians in an overwhelmingly non-Christian setting; and the irrelevance of many of the European and American divisions apart from the geographical areas where they developed.

This period of the Reformed Church's history closes with the church no nearer organic union with any church than it was in the beginning, although it considered many possible schemes for union. It was, however, much more heavily involved in cooperative and federative work, such as the Federal Council of Churches and the Reformed and Presbyterian Alliance. It had also moved forward from the concept of Reformed-Presbyterian union overseas to a conviction that only comprehensive Protestant church union would meet the crucial needs of other lands.

VII
Cross-Currents (1930-1960)

Opposition to the Federal Council

This period of the Reformed Church's history opens soon after the outbreak of open war between the "fundamentalists" and the "modernists" in many denominations. The battle was particularly severe in the sister Presbyterian Church, which had removed Harry Emerson Fosdick as "stated supply" preacher in the First Presbyterian Church of New York City only a few years before.[1] It had also seen, in 1929, the organization of a new "fundamentalist" seminary in Philadelphia under the leadership of J. Gresham Machen. Within the Reformed Church the struggle did not reach battle proportions, no ministers were removed on either side, no organizational breaks occurred. But the growing Western, conservative element had clear sympathies with the "fundamentalist" cause, and had hopes of getting the Reformed Church as a whole to espouse it. The early part of the period thus saw a growing tide of reaction, a tide which was unable to cause the church as a whole to move in its direction, but which was able to prevent change in any other direction.

One of the chief objects of attack by the conservatives was the Federal Council of Churches, and it remained throughout this period a conservative aim to have the Reformed Church withdraw from the Council. The attack was opened on the 1930 Lenten devotional booklet put out by the Federal Council, called the "Fellowship of Prayer." "It is," wrote a Western pastor in the church paper, "simply Unitarian from the first page to the last."[2] He described the booklet's discussion of themes such as "Coming to Terms with the Universe," "Coming to Terms with Ourselves," and "Coming to Terms with Ultimate Things." The booklet didn't require one to come to terms with God, the writer went on, and made no reference to Christ as divine. "If this is a sample of what the Federal Council of Churches wants the Christian Churches in the country to believe and to live by," he concluded, "then it is another reason for breaking connections with them."[3]

Many Western churchmen agreed, and the 1930 General Synod received overtures from nine classes and one of the two Western particular synods, protesting the distribution of the "Fellowship of Prayer." Under a conservative chairman, the Overtures Committee recommended that the next year's pamphlet be carefully scrutinized for doctrinal accuracy, and that it not be distributed if found wanting.[4] Apparently there was no improvement in the 1931 edition, from the conservative point of view, because again the Western classes, and the two Western synods, sent in numerous overtures. This time, however, there appeared the first requests that relations with the Federal Council be severed. Reasons for withdrawal included "the prominence of certain non-evangelical leaders in the work and activities of the Council," "modernistic tendencies revealed in both the preaching of its official spokesman as also in its official publications," and its pronouncement on birth control.[5] The Overtures Committee, now under a more liberal chairman, recommended that "Fellowship of Prayer" emphasize the evangelical Lenten accents. It then proceeded to detail the extensive work done by the Council which could not be done by individual denominations, and its recommendation that the Reformed Church "continue in active participation in the Federal Council" was adopted by the Synod.[6] Further overtures of complaint and requests for withdrawal arose in 1933 and 1934, but the Committee's reply, adopted by Synod, seems to have been accepted for a decade or so as definitive:

Pronouncements subject to such disapproval have been rare, however, and have been particularly the expression of a committee rather than of the Council as a whole. The Council on the other hand represents the united Protestant Churches of America in the great Christian enterprise of the Kingdom of God in many important ways and it would not be appropriate for the Reformed Church in America to be dissociated from it or to fail to support it if still connected with it.[7]

The Committee saw fit also to include a word of warning to the Council itself:

A rising tide of protest makes it imperative to insist on our denominational loyalty to our Reformed Church doctrinal position and to give notice that there is a point beyond which cooperation cannot go. There are places where, in the judgment of Reformed Church people, Christ is wounded in the house of His friends and the Reformed Church in America does not propose to stay in such a house.[8]

The coming of the Second World War and the need for solidarity and unity, as well as the concrete evidence during the War of what the Federal Council was able to do that denominations could not do, may have helped to stave off criticism for a time. But early in 1947 the Rev. Henry Bast, a Western minister, sent out a printed pamphlet entitled, *An Appeal to the Ministers and Laymen of the Chicago and Iowa Synods.*[9] In it Bast attacked the Federal Council of Churches, the International Council of Religious Education, the New Brunswick Theological Seminary, Hope College, the Boards of the denomination, the level of giving of the eastern synods to benevolent causes, and the missionaries being appointed to overseas positions. He urged that overtures be sent asking for withdrawal from the Federal Council and the International Council of Religious Education because "the most notorious liberals in Protestantism are in these councils, and in the leadership of these councils."[10] He also urged overtures calling for the headquarters of the church to be moved from New York to the Midwest, because the two western synods gave 71% of the denomination's benevolent money in 1946. New Brunswick Seminary was charged with doctrinal indifference because it had on its faculty "a man from Union Seminary in New York City, who, although he has not been called to the professorship, is still teaching the students at New Brunswick the Old Testament."[11] That, in his view, was proof enough:

Where is a denomination going which cooperates with all of the liberal organizations of Protestantism and none of the conservative organizations, that has at least one seminary and one college in a very serious condition in regard to faith, and whose Boards are controlled by one area of the church in which there is not enough spiritual life to make a reasonable contribution to the benevolent work of that church?

This is a dark picture. It is not overdrawn. The inroads that worldliness and indifference have made into our churches are greater than can be put down in such an objective statement of facts.[12]

The extent of Bast's influence in the West is indicated by the fact that the 1947 General Synod was greeted with five overtures having to do with Board membership, eleven regarding re-location of church headquarters in the West, eleven against continued membership in the Federal Council, and three against continued membership in the International Council of Religious Education.[13] His negative influence in the East is also indicated by several overtures critical of the *Church Herald*, which published some of Bast's material, and of whose editorial council he was a member. In reply to the overtures critical of Bast for his "unfair criticisms of the Boards and institutions of the church,"[14] the committee "expressed regrets because of the unhappy developments," but felt that "sheer Christianity and church policy demand that the church take the shock of the experience and that we all 'go forward'."[15] To answer the other overtures, Synod set up two special committees, one to study the matter of affiliation with the Federal Council and the other to study the matter of location of headquarters.

During the year following, the chairman of the special committee, assigned to evaluate the present relation to the Federal Council and contrast it with possible membership in the National Association of Evangelicals, was in correspondence with many people in an attempt to give a fair report. Dr. Albertus Pieters, the former missionary to Japan and professor at Western Seminary, was for withdrawal:

> Every man and every organization having definite scriptural and evangelical convictions should take sides in the conflict between Modernism and the Christian faith. . . . In addition to the doctrinal convictions involved, I think withdrawal is for us at present also the path of highest expediency. I can think of nothing that would more greatly unify our denomination. . .[16]

When questioned as to how withdrawal would unify the denomination, Dr. Pieters admitted that he had been looking at the matter from one side only, the western one, and that he was "not well informed how strongly those in the East feel about it."[17]

Early in 1948 a group of Reformed church ministers and laymen calling themselves the "Evangelical Brotherhood" met in Chicago, and after reaffirming their faith in the Bible as the "inspired and infallible Word of God," they pledged themselves to support only such interdenominational fellowship and cooperation as agreed with the Reformed Standards of Faith, which they understood as requiring that cooperative groups "publicly affirm the authority of the Bible as the infallible Word of God and the only rule of faith and practice."[18] An executive of the denomination, heavily involved in interdenominational cooperation, attended as an observer, and later remarked on the attitude of suspicion in the meeting:

> There has always been a suspicion held by some that there were ministers in other sections of the church who held unorthodox views

and who denied some of the cardinal doctrines of the Christian faith. At General Synod last spring, it was reported, some of these brethren were present and gave expression to these heretical views, declaring they did not believe in the Virgin Birth of Christ, the Atonement, and the physical resurrection. Those who held the suspicion were now confirmed in their lack of confidence in these other brethren, and since there were those in our midst who denied essential elements of our faith, something should be done."[19]

Later that spring the professors of the two seminaries devised a plan to halt the withdrawal—they prepared an open letter, favoring the Federal Council, and sent it to all pastors, asking them to read it to their congregations. In it they urged continued membership because the Reformed Church was a charter member, Protestants needed a cooperative organization, and the forty years of membership had vindicated the Council inasmuch as it helped the denomination do its work and gave it opportunities for service.[20] The response from the East was highly favorable to the letter; in the West there was considerable criticism, especially of the Western Seminary faculty. The president of New Brunswick wrote to the president of Western: "Keep a stout heart."[21]

The tactic, along with a great deal of hard work trying to convince people, paid off at the General Synod of 1948. All but one member of the special committee came out for continued membership in the Council. A minority report was presented by the dissident member of the committee, the Rev. Lawrence Borst, calling for withdrawal from the Council because of "modernism." There were extensive quotes from an article Bast wrote which appeared in Carl McIntire's *Christian Beacon* in March 1948, including this accusation by Bast (not, however, credited to Bast by Borst): "Since 1934 [when the previous attempt was made to get the Reformed Church out of the Council], Oxnam has made his notorious slurring remark on the Old Testament, and Fosdick has made his belligerent denial of the Virgin Birth and the Substitutionary Atonement."[22] The attempt to approve the minority report failed by a roll call vote of 151-65, and the majority report was adopted.

The Reformed Church voted its intent to become a member of the World Council of Churches in 1937, and one of its members, the Rev. A. Livingston Warnshuis, helped to write the constitution of the World Council. In 1948, when the World Council became a reality in Amsterdam, the Reformed Church was a charter member. In 1950, when the Federal Council of Churches and seven other major interdenominational agencies combined to form the National Council of Churches of Christ in the U. S. A., the Reformed Church was also a charter member. The change of name from Federal Council to National Council, along with change of some personnel, tended to reduce opposition within the Reformed Church. However, when in the late 1950's anti-Communism became a fad in certain areas of the country, this became a weapon for some to use against both the National and World Councils. Each year from 1958 to 1963 saw several overtures from Western classes, alleging some kind of Communist taint in the World and/or National Councils.[23] Later the focus of attack shifted from "Communist taint" to a concern about pronouncements on social issues. These movements have never had the strength that the 1947-8 effort did, and it would seem that the majority of members expect that the Reformed Church is now committed to membership in these ecumenical organizations.

Romig & Baptism

The difference between the Eastern and Western sections of the church, and the difference in approach on matters ecumenical and theological, reached its apex in the 1940's. In his State of Religion address in 1941 as president of the General Synod, Dr. Edgar F. Romig of the Collegiate Church of New York said, among other things:

Traditionalist that I am, I could no more in the Baptism Office ask parents to subscribe to the question, "Do you believe that our children are sinful and guilty before God?" than I could ask them to believe in Mohammed. For I cannot find warrant in Scripture for any doctrine that children whose wills have not yet been formed and who therefore cannot exercise the power of moral choice are guilty before God. Has not the hour struck for us courageously to depart from lawlessness by giving thought to modified forms?[24]

A month later the theological argument had been begun in the church paper by a Western pastor, declaring that in the above statement Dr. Romig "has disavowed the Reformed Doctrine of Original Sin" and that he "has disavowed the Biblical basis for that doctrine in its application to infants."[25] The same writer was correspondent for a Christian Reformed paper, and let them in on the family argument, stating that though Romig had written extensively "in an effort to clear himself of any unfavourable charge," it was questionable whether he succeeded. In addition, he told the Chris-

tian Reformed of "another disturbance," centering around Dr.
Norman Vincent Peale, who served during the summer of 1941 as
technical advisor in Hollywood for Warner Brothers' movie, "One
Foot in Heaven." "Some of us," he continued,

> are of the opinion that a minister in the Reformed Church in
> America has, to put it bluntly, no business in Hollywood. From the
> point of view of their psychological effects it is unfortunate that
> both of these controversies were occasioned by brethren in the
> eastern section of our church.[26]

Neither of the two matters was an occasion of controversy, of
course, until this particular pastor began to suggest that they should
be.

Almost no one followed through on the attack on Peale, but
rumblings of the Romig remarks continued throughout the year.
Dr. R. B. Kuiper, one-time Reformed Churchman who had since
joined the Orthodox Presbyterian Church and their Westminster
Seminary faculty, harked back to 1923 in his attack:

> A most serious issue confronts the Reformed Church in America.
> This writer said recently that, if history should repeat itself, the
> church would do nothing, or next to nothing, about it. That state-
> ment must stand, for it is a fact that in 1923 Dr. Edward S. Wor-
> cester's bold denial of the Reformed doctrine of original sin did not
> prevent his election to the chair of Systematic Theology at the New
> Brunswick Theological Seminary. But the good news may be added
> that the cloud the size of a man's hand which appeared immedi-
> ately upon the publication of Dr. Romig's report, in the form of a
> public protest against his view of original sin, has since been
> growing. . . . The Reformed Church in America is indeed on trial.[27]

This attack from outside was resented by Reformed Churchmen,
especially as Kuiper had previously attacked the Reformed Church
in a book called *As to Being Reformed.* One pastor, recalling that
fact, asked:

> What, then, is the motive? We need harbor no illusions on that
> score. Here is a deliberate attempt to promote discord and dis-
> affection in our church. . . . A man who has no conscientious scruples
> about aiding and abetting the malignant forces that have caused
> disruption in our sister denomination, the Presbyterian Church,
> will have none about doing the same in our Church.[28]

The uproar continued, however, and at one point Romig wrote to his friend Dr. John W. Beardslee, Jr., at New Brunswick Seminary: "Taken as a whole, they [the materials on the controversy] are something of a revelation of American religious thought in this year of grace, 1941."[29] Beardslee, in reply, wrote: "The more I read and hear of this lamentable debate, the more angry I become. I am sorry for myself, because it becomes more and more impossible for me to talk sincerely on the subject."[30]

Because a minister can be disciplined only by his own classis, the Classis of West Sioux (Iowa) sent communications to all classes in the denomination, asking them to protest against Romig in order to "prevent as much as possible the Sacraments from being profaned . . . and that no strange doctrine be taught in our church."[31] A number of western classes did overture General Synod to take action to protect the doctrinal standards. But a number of eastern classes protested the action of the Classis of West Sioux, saying they had proceeded unconstitutionally and in an un-Christian manner, by calling Romig heretical without his being proven so.[32] They also requested that the Liturgy be revised to eliminate that against which Romig had protested. As the outsider, Kuiper, predicted, the Reformed Church did next to nothing—it reaffirmed the church's belief in its doctrinal standards, and referred the requests for changes in the liturgy to the Committee on Revision of the Liturgy.[33] Thus, in spite of the wide-spread agitation, the sizeable conservative minority was unable to achieve the action it desired.

MacLean and the Canaanites

Toward the end of the forties, the conservatives were more successful. In his inaugural address as professor of Old Testament at New Brunswick Seminary, Dr. Hugh Baillie MacLean spoke on the meaning and relevance of the Old Testament for the church today. Among other points which he made, this one was singled out by critics in the West:

Wholesale and ruthless extermination of people is attributed by the writers to God's expressed command. Our minds and consciences today revolt at the wanton destruction attributed, for example, to Joshua in his conquest of the Promised Land. But the explanation lies in the date of these conquest narratives and the background against which they were written. As the Deuteronomic writers saw the picture at the end of the seventh century

B.C., with the northern kingdom of Israel in exile and the southern kingdom of Judah threatened with imminent destruction, they concluded that the root cause was the secularization of life and religion through contact with the local inhabitants of Canaan. Thus they rewrote the history of Israel with this philosophy in mind . . . History may have been falsified in the interests of philosophy but the moral lesson is still true.[34]

The point of view of those critical of MacLean's address is typified in this letter to the editor of the church paper:

Since when has it been Reformed to deny the veracity, the truthfulness of the history of God's Word upon which our Reformed concepts of spiritual truth is [sic] built? . . . If such a thing [that the Bible contains false history] is assumed, and it is just an assumption which is not based on objective scholarship, that man deliberately and falsely attributed to God those words which he never uttered, how can I be assured that this same thing may not be true of those other words in the Bible which instill holy aspirations and high hopes into my soul concerning my eternal destiny with God in Christ? . . . Do you think that the Holy Spirit would lend Himself to a falsification of history?[35]

Others picked up this complaint, and kept it alive throughout the year, necessitating action at the General Synod of 1949. This was what the president of New Brunswick had had a premonition about a year earlier, after the seminary faculties had come out for the Federal Council. He wrote then to the president of Western Seminary:

There is just one anxiety which I carry and that is with reference to the vote of the General Synod to call Dr. Hugh B. MacLean to the Chair of Old Testament, in our Seminary. It may be that this small group will try to maneuver a motion that we either lay this on the table or that we take no action. That, of course, would be fatal for us. . . . I hope that some of you brethren in the west will not countenance any such possibility.[36]

The 1949 Synod received thirty-three communications about Dr. MacLean (there were only 42 classes at the time). Thirteen overtures from Western classes and the two Western particular synods opposed MacLean, calling for further explanation of his views and how they related to the doctrinal standards. Seventeen overtures from Eastern classes and two Eastern particular synods expressed confidence in MacLean. Dr. MacLean made an explanation of his beliefs, in which he affirmed the inspiration of the Scriptures without espousing any particular theory of inspiration; he accepted the record of the extermination of the Canaanites, as within the will of God, though not a final or adequate expression of God's will; he explained that when he spoke of "falsification" of history, he was merely emphasizing that history is "fact plus interpretation." This satisfied a majority of the Synod, which expressed its confidence in Dr. MacLean.[37]

The United Presbyterian Church of North America

The controversy about Dr. MacLean and the Federal Council controversy both played a part in the defeat of the one major effort toward organic union in this period, which also occurred in the 1940's. So little interest in organic union was evinced during the 1930's that in 1937 the Committee on Closer Relations with Other Denominations was disbanded.[38] The next year, when a particular synod overtured General Synod to consider union with the Evangelical and Reformed Church, the Synod voted that "the present time is not propitious for taking aggressive action toward organic union."[39] But by 1945 the newly-constituted "Permanent Committee on Fraternal Relations with Other Denominations" of the General Synod felt that "in the light of the world movement toward world unity, economically, politically, and ecclesiastically, the subject [of church union] deserves fresh approach and new treatment."[40] The possibilities of the Presbyterian Church, U. S. A., and the Evangelical and Reformed Church were considered, but in light of an invitation from the United Presbyterian Church, the committee suggested that conversations be initiated with them. The United Presbyterian Church of North America was about the same size as the Reformed Church, and the two groups did not overlap geographically. Both represented a somewhat conservative Calvinism. Union would widen horizons, bring new vitality, and further demonstrate to the world the Church's love and unity.[41]

At the first exploratory meeting, between representatives of the Reformed and United Presbyterian Churches, few differences were found. "The matter of social customs, dancing, movies, playing cards, etc. was discussed at some length. It was finally felt that these matters should not enter into our consideration since neither Church had ever made a definite pronouncement on these matters."[42] This became a bone of contention much later in the discussions, though it was not mentioned again for quite some time. In February 1946, at the second meeting of the committee, a letter was read from the large Presbyterian Church in the U. S. A., asking for further union. Members of the committee from both smaller churches answered that "any discussion of further union might jeopardize the proposed union between our two churches."[43]

The committee's first task was to acquaint the two denominations with each other, which was done by a series of articles on the history, polity, theology, missions, liturgy, education, pension plans, etc., of the two denominations in both church papers, which appeared monthly from April 1946 to March 1947. Following that, the articles were published in a pamphlet entitled *Digest of Facts,* and distributed widely.[44] A plan of union was also prepared, under the chairmanship of the Rev. M. Stephen James of New Brunswick Seminary. The committee noted that "when differences were expressed in the Joint Committee they seldom followed denominational lines, but almost invariably crossed and recrossed those lines."[45] This plan of union, in accord with committee vote, named the proposed new church "The United Presbyterian Reformed Church."[46] In light of protests calling for a shorter name, it was reduced for a time to "Presbyterian Reformed Church," but later changed back again.[47]

A discussion of the merits of the proposed union began in the church paper early in 1947. One Western minister opposed union on these three grounds: loss of denominational distinctiveness; theological weakness in the United Presbyterian Church; and differences in practise. But in this last item he lumped together such diverse elements as the question of liturgy, Dutch Reformed opposition to dancing, and Dutch Reformed opposition to Free Masonry.[48] Another Western minister opposed union with the United Presbyterians because of two items in their Confessional Statement of 1925. They called the Scriptures "*an* infallible rule of faith and practice" instead of "*the* infallible rule."[49] Also, they advocated "forbearance in love" for those who are unable fully to agree with the doctrinal standards. These two statements indicated the existence of liberalism and tolerance of heresy in that church, as far as this writer was concerned.[50] In reply, a member of the committee suggested that "the statement as it stands does not teach that the Bible is one of many infallible rules. To reach that conclusion one must get it by an implication which never was intended. . . . As I read the study of Brother Fikse I keep asking myself whether he is trying to make the best interpretation or the worst."[51]

One Western minister admitted that his concern was frankly one of political power. By union

> you weaken the hands of the conservative and more than proportionately strengthen the hands of the liberals. Liberalism flourishes much more in large bodies than small bodies. The smaller denominations, perhaps with an exception here and there, have disproportionately much less liberalism than the larger denominations. And the first thing that liberalism attempts is to get into the boards and educational institutions of a denomination. This needs no argument, for it is a matter of history.[52]

The note of suspicion heard earlier, and the determination to put the worst possible construction on the proposed union, are evident here. "Liberalism" is regarded as an organized force seeking control, rather than as a point of view contending for truth along with other points of view.

The joint committee's report to the 1947 Synod was enthusiastic about the value of union, noting that although "many of us came to the union proposition with considerable misgivings as to the benefits to be gained through union with another denomination, we now find ourselves, after three years of negotiations, all favorably disposed toward this proposed union."[53] In view of the fact that this committee included many Western conservatives, this was seen as a hopeful statement, and the Synod voted to have a full-scale plan of union prepared, published, and distributed. This was done in 1948, as an enlarged version of the original plan of 1946. Classes were asked to study this proposal and make suggestions for the final Plan of Union, to be published in 1949, upon which the ultimate vote would be taken.

The Classis of Grand Rapids, one of the strongest classes in the West, spoke for many Western classes in its objections to the Plan of Union. Instead of the constitutionally required majority vote in two-thirds of the classes for approval of the plan, Grand Rapids asked for a required ¾ majority vote in a total of ¾ of the classes. The Classis also objected to the statement urging that forbearance in love be exercised toward those who couldn't fully subscribe to the doctrinal standards, a statement taken from the United Presbyterian Confessional Statement. Recognizing that some good might come from union, the Classis alleged that negative factors included the United Presbyterian intention of further union, the lack of enthusiasm among the Reformed, the lack of provision for dissenting congregations, and the idea that people interested in ecumenical matters trusted in numbers rather than the Holy Spirit. The Classis saw no need to unite, believing that spiritual unity was sufficient.[54]

The discussion of the union proposal was also carried on throughout the year 1949, both before and after the final "Plan of Union" appeared. An article, either pro or con, appeared almost every week in the church paper. The Rev. Albertus Pieters, now retired from Western Seminary, used much the same arguments against union that he had against union with the Presbyterian Church in 1930. "Why should we not unite with the United Presbyterian Church? I know of no good answer to that question." He saw no danger to evangelical Christianity. The question "Why shouldn't we unite?" he said, "has not been answered, and cannot be."[55] But the more important question to him remained, "Why should we unite?" Many people, he felt, were victims of "unionitis dogmaticus," considering disunion a sin and shame, and quoting John 17.21; which, he said, "gives me a pain."[56]

In reply the Rev. M. Verne Oggel, for many years a Presbyterian, suggested that Pieters' preference for a oneness of faith and love without organizational unity was a Unitarian aberration, because Christian orthodoxy insisted that Christ was "of one substance with the Father." If the church were to be one like Christ and the Father were, it would require organic union. Pieters had disdained those who spoke of union as "the will of God" as claiming special revelation. Oggel answered:

This is hardly a situation where a devout Churchman who has come, perhaps after a struggle, to believe that the proposed union is 'according to the will of God and the mind of Christ' should be sneered at for talking as though 'he has a special revelation on the subject.' This whole attempt to play down the relevancy of high Christian decision amazes one by its cynicism.

It makes you wonder whether Dr. Pieters is not actually allergic to this union—if not to any union—for dispositional reasons and *therefore* seeks to reduce consideration of the issue to an a-Christian level from which a denomination could never be lifted to the spiritual height required to launch a significant Christian advance.[57]

Oggel also had words for those who wanted to keep the denomination as it was for personal reasons:

The opposition to this union among our people is, at bottom, an emotional preference for keeping our denomination as it is—a big family of a certain national origin. I must confess I sympathize with this preference. After an absence from the Reformed fold of a quarter of a century, I am deeply sensible of the charms of this pleasant, homey fellowship, where everybody more or less knows everybody else. Nevertheless, the moment this preference militates against the achievement of a wider Christian unity, it ceases to be an innocent sentiment and must come under the judgement of Him who by His cross destroys middle walls of partition.[58]

Remarkable as it may seem, the arguments used for union were based, by and large, on Biblical and theological grounds, the arguments against union on emotional attitudes and non-theological grounds. Those favoring union spoke of Christ's concern for the unity of his body, the Church; of the need for organic union so that the world might see and believe; and of their desire to take this step so that at least one division in the visible body of Christ might be overcome. Those who opposed union tended to base their opposition on a concern for the Dutch heritage, a fear that their position would lose political strength in the united church, anxiety over the introduction of social customs which were alien to their peculiar tradition (though found in many areas of the Reformed Church), and a desire not to give up the comfortable status quo with its "all-one-happy-family" aspects. This was in spite of the opposition's claim to be more Biblically-oriented than the advocates of union. The Rev. Lester Kuyper of Western Seminary was heartily in favor of union, saying that "the cause of disunity in the Church is sin."[59] The Rev. Samuel M. Zwemer, long time Arabian missionary and later professor at Princeton, urged union because it would strengthen missions, concern for the Sabbath, stewardship, theological education, and would give a wider forum for the Calvinistic interpretation of the gospel.[60] The Stated Clerk of the denomination asked a vital question:

Perhaps there are things which could be accomplished through cooperation, but as a matter of cold fact we have not thus cooperated down through the years. In all sincerity, how many of us were even vaguely conscious of the existence of the United Presbyterian Church to say nothing about our willingness to cooperate with them in the building of the Kingdom of God?[61]

Oggel, in a final article for union, spoke of those who wanted to look far into the future:

Take the man who asks nervously, 'What will this union lead to? What will be the next step, and the next?' The answer is that, for the Christian, obedience is always an *ad hoc* affair. 'I do not ask to see the distant scene, One step enough for me.'[62]

He went on to point out that Jesus prayed for unity among his followers "that the world might believe," and because the world looks at outward appearances and judges by externals, spiritual unity alone can not fulfill the requirements of this prayer.[63]

On the other side of the question, one Western minister argued, extra-theologically, that

The law of denominations is the law of nations. It may seem grand to fly around the world in a day or two and write a book, as Mr. Wilkie [sic] did, about *One World*. But your One World will be happier and saner and safer as a family of nations; and none of them big, for they easily become haughty, like U. S. S. R. and U. S. Such is equally applicable to the Church.[64]

A number of Western laymen also wrote opposing union, and argued that schism was likely if union were pursued. After pointing out that some Congregational churches were setting up an independent organization, one wrote:

Now, brethren, I am sure we would not want this to happen to our beloved Church, and we westerners know it could happen. I would not be surprised if it would make a split in the Reformed Church of [sic] America.[65]

The Rev. Henry Bast claimed that Scripture had nothing to say about union. "To quote some text out of the Bible, as if that text is authoritative from the Word of God to approve this merger, is to misuse the Bible."[66] The real questions, he said, were: What view of the Bible will prevail in the educational work of the united church? Will the new denomination be congregational or presbyterian? He suspected that plenary inspiration would not be taught, and that the new church would be congregational in doctrine and presbyterian in administration. "What makes a denomination?" he asked, and his answer was: agreement in doctrine.[67] He ignored the fact that differences of doctrine within each of the two denominations were greater than those between the two.

The final Plan of Union of 1949 was a comprehensive and well-written document. It included a summary statement of doctrine, a complete constitution and book of worship, legal opinions on the union, and the enabling act. The doctrinal summary was in agreement with the standards of the two churches. The governmental structure of the new church would be along classic presbyterian lines, with the terms of the United Presbyterian Church generally used instead of the comparable Reformed ones. The Liturgy was essentially the Liturgy of the Reformed Church, but the Plan did not make its use compulsory. No legal obstacles were foreseen in uniting the two churches. The final plan provided for a "three-fourths majority vote in the Classes and Presbyteries and a three-fourths majority of the total number of Classes and Presbyteries in each denomination."[68]

The votes of the classes and presbyteries came in between January and June of 1950. The percentage of approval ranged from 4% in the Classis of Muskegon (Michigan) to 100% in about a third of the Eastern classes. Only three Eastern classes gave less than 50% approval—they were in two cases classes with large 19th Century Dutch constituencies, and in the third possessed of a leader who opposed union on liturgical grounds. On the other hand, no Western classis gave more than 50% approval to the plan. Twenty-four of forty-two classes gave majority approval, but only nineteen gave the required 75% approval. Thus the plan failed and was not ratified by the 1950 Synod, even though a majority of the classes and a majority of those voting approved it.

In the United Presbyterian Church, the majority for union was much stronger. Eighty-five percent of those voting were for union, yet the United Presbyterians failed to give the required double three-fourths majority. Dr. Wallace Jamison, author of the United Presbyterian centennial history, points out that under the "double three-quarters" scheme, a properly-spaced 4% negative vote could have defeated the Plan. Jamison believed that "the Dutch heritage was still too precious to risk dissipating it in a union with the Scotch-Irish."[69] Eight years later the United Presbyterians had joined with the Presbyterian Church in the U. S. A. to form the new "United Presbyterian Church in the U. S. A."

And the Reformed Church continued to stand alone. Dr. Luman J. Shafer, a prominent Reformed Church minister, former missionary, and missions executive, who was co-chairman of the joint committee working for union, said of the negative vote, "This has set the Reformed Church back 100 years."[70]

VIII
Future Prospects

A number of conclusions may be drawn from this study of the ecumenical relations of the Reformed Church, and the contrast between her positive expressions of Christian unity and her negative actions in regard to church union with other members of the Reformed-Presbyterian family. The overall impression given by the Reformed faith in general and the Reformed Church in America in particular is one of a strong ecumenical interest and impulse. Neither Calvin nor his followers claimed exclusive possession of the truth; the Reformed Church has never regarded herself as the only true church.

The Dutch Reformed Church, both in the Netherlands and in this country, recognized from an early date the essential oneness of the Reformed and Presbyterian branches of Calvinism. The proposal of 1743 which would have united Dutch and German Reformed and Scots Presbyterians could come only from a recognition of basic unity. The desire to establish herself as an organization and to protect her Dutch language and heritage kept the Dutch Reformed Church from early union. The language barrier was a real barrier, even if maintained longer than necessary. Once the language problem had disappeared, many recognized that the chief *raison d'etre* of the Dutch Church had also disappeared.

Recognition that the Dutch Reformed Church did not hold a unique theological position was shown in her approach to overseas mission work. She began such work interdenominationally, through the American Board of Commissioners for Foreign Missions. She later set up her own overseas board, but chiefly as a technique for raising more money. By 1864, more than a century ago, she was firmly committed to united indigenous churches overseas. In spite of minority opinion to the contrary, she has continued to follow that policy with steadfast determination. Today she works in Africa with the Church of Christ in the Upper Nile; in India with the Church of South India; in Japan with the United Church of Christ in Japan; among Chinese with the United Church of Christ in the Philippines, the Hong Kong Council of the Church of Christ in China, the Presbyterian Church of Formosa, and the Malaya-

Singapore Synod of the Chinese Christian Church; and in Mexico with the Presbyterian Church in Mexico. Her work in Arabia and Iraq, still in mission stage, is part of a united Presbyterian mission.

The Reformed Church also recognized how much she had in common with other Christian bodies by being active in cooperative councils in the United States and in the world. She was a charter member of the Federal Council of Churches and its successor, the National Council of Churches of Christ in the U. S. A. She cooperated in ecumenical mission conferences, and became a charter member of the World Council of Churches in 1948. Her local churches and synods are active in local, county, and state councils of churches. She is also a member of the Alliance of Reformed Churches Throughout the World Holding the Presbyterian Order.*

That the church had come to realize the implications of her essential unity with other Reformed and Presbyterian bodies is evident from the numerous proposals for union which came before her over the years. By the end of the nineteenth century, the required majority of classes actually approved the proposal for union with the German Reformed Church. By that time, however, a new element had been injected into the situation—the nineteenth-century Dutch immigration. This body with its secessionist-separatist background in the Netherlands joined the older Dutch Reformed body, then prevented the merger by using the threat of secession. This threat carried weight because some of the Western Dutch had already seceded. Rather than split the church, the majority yielded to the minority.

That decision to yield to the minority has since plagued the ecumenically-minded wing of the church. The element with the secessionist background has grown in strength until it numbers about half of the denomination. Located primarily in the Western non-urban areas of the country, it has kept to itself, frequently in small Dutch enclaves. It has been able to prevent any twentieth-century proposals for union from reaching fruition. While its opposition to union is often couched in theological terms, and while it claims to be truer to the Bible than the ecumenical group, non-theological factors carry the greatest weight. Among them are the Dutch heritage and tradition, and doubts about the non-Dutch; the "come-outer" separatist tradition, which thinks in terms of dividing rather than uniting; a contentment with the status quo

*When the Alliance unites with the International Congregational Council in 1970, its official name will be "The World Alliance of Reformed Churches (Presbyterian and Congregational)."

made possible by isolation from mainstream America. In addition, since the time of the fundamentalist-modernist controversy in the 1920's, a minority which espouses both Biblical and creedal fundamentalism has feared contact with anyone who differs even in minor details.

The anti-ecumenical, or a-ecumenical, factor in the church is not strong enough to cause the Reformed Church to withdraw from its present ecumenical endeavors in this country and overseas, for that would require a clear majority. But because at least a two-thirds majority would be required for any church union, it has had, at least until recently, sufficient strength to prevent any union from taking place.

Prospects for the future of the Reformed Church, with emphasis on its ecumenical stance, would seem to include three possible alternatives:

I. She can attempt to maintain the status quo, remaining separate as she has for the past three centuries. The likely result of such action would be the withering away of the Reformed Church in the metropolitan areas of the East. The membership of the eastern part of the church has remained about the same for a number of years, because most of the eastern churches are in the metropolitan area, where Protestants are a minority and the Reformed Church relatively unknown. This reduction in the East could lead to a greater dominance of the West with consequent growth of conservatism.

II. It is possible that before the first alternative could happen, there would be a division between the Eastern and Western branches of the Reformed Church. Many ministers in the East would like to see their congregations leave the Reformed Church, if she refuses to unite with the Presbyterians, and become Presbyterian themselves. The historic Reformed Church as such would then be destroyed, with the Western section continuing alone as a conservative body, or possibly joining the Christian Reformed Church.

III. The third, and best, alternative would become possible if the Western element of the Reformed Church were gradually to become more involved in the mainstream of American life, take a more responsible attitude toward the nation as a whole, and become interested in joining forces with another like-minded denomination. There are signs that this best alternative may be the one eventually chosen.

The Rev. M. Verne Oggel wrote a letter to the church paper

in May 1961, suggesting that the Reformed Church explore the possibilities of union with the Presbyterian Church in the U. S. (Southern), rather than follow the lead of a number of overtures calling for union with the United Presbyterian Church.[1] The Reformed Church must, he felt, consider some movement toward union, and the Southern Presbyterians seemed to him closer to the Reformed in terms of conservatism, mission work, per capita giving, and general outlook. They were also small enough that the Reformed Church would not be swallowed up, and geographically the two churches compliment each other, the one being entirely in the South and the other in the North.[2]

A number of classes picked up Oggel's suggestion and overtured the 1961 General Synod to initiate conversations with the Southern Presbyterians. Synod's committee on overtures was afraid of any specific negotiations, and considered them premature. The committee recommended no action except to turn all documents pertaining to church union over to the newly-formed Executive Committee. A motion from the floor asking the Executive Committee to hold conversations with both Presbyterian bodies was approved.[3]

The Executive Committee's conversations with the United Presbyterian Church were friendly, but because of the Consultation on Church Union (involving a number of denominations) no further steps were recommended. The discussion with the Southern Presbyterians, however, brought forth a joint resolution, harking back to close relations begun in 1874, and calling for common exploration of 14 areas of common concern. These 14 areas included doctrine and polity, worship and liturgy, world missions, education, evangelism, church extension, stewardship, and Christian action. To explore these areas, General Synod appointed a special committee of twelve to meet with a similar Southern Presbyterian committee.[4] In addition the committee on overtures recommended that the Executive Committee "take steps looking toward merger with the Presbyterian Church in the U.S.,"[5] a recommendation which Synod approved.

The Joint Committee of Twenty-Four has met frequently since its appointment in 1962, and annual reports have been made to the General Synod and to the General Assembly of the Presbyterian Church in the United States. At the first meeting subcommittees were appointed to study (a) doctrine, liturgy and Christian action; (b) polity and organizational structure; and (c) cooperative relations between program boards and agencies, and personnel exchanges for mutual acquaintance.[6] The subcommittee on doctrine had a statement prepared on "The Witness of the Reformed Churches," which after stating the virtual identity of theology in the doctrinal standards of the two denominations, affirmed that "in a very real sense we have nothing distinctive to say and we rejoice in this admission. For it has always been the claim of the Reformed churches that they are part of the holy catholic church and stand in the great tradition of the historic Christian faith. We begin, therefore, with the assertion that the Reformed witness is a witness to the catholic faith."[7] The Reformed churches have, however, the report maintained, spoken the faith with a particular accent; that is, with particular stress on the sovereignty of God, the authority of Scripture, and obedience to the will of God. The theological statement was approved by both the General Synod and the General Assembly in 1964.

It was also in its report to the 1964 synod and assembly that the Joint Committee first mentioned the possibility of organic union. The committee had originally planned to ask for a federation, realizing that "cooperation" was not enough, but eventually it recognized that it must go further, and thus recommended:

We make these (prior) recommendations with the realization that they are fragmented and incomplete unless seen in the context of a larger purpose and direction. We wish now to say that we have had candid and extended discussions and have made lengthy and detailed studies. We have found such large areas of agreement in theology, worship, and polity that we have been led to the conclusion that there are no major impediments between our two denominations in these basic fields.

If, therefore, the practical problems of our separate life and work can be resolved through these and other studies and if our conviction is correct that we can witness to the Gospel, and especially to the Reformation emphasis on the authority of Scripture and the Sovereignty of God as expressed in the Lordship of Jesus Christ, more effectively together than we can separately, we affirm prayerfully and hopefully that we envision the union of our two churches. We believe that the varied patterns of ethnic, regional and historical identities which are found within both our denominations will be enriched and more mightily used for the Kingdom's work within the larger context of faith and witness that such a union would bring.

We therefore recommend that the General Assembly and the General Synod instruct the Joint Committee of Twenty-Four and the several Boards and Agencies . . . to consider "a more effective witness" as the focus of these joint studies and the possibility of the union of our two churches as the framework of suggested action.[8]

This recommendation was also adopted by both the General Synod and the General Assembly in 1964.

By the time of the 1965 General Synod, three major documents had been prepared, comparing the constitutions of the two churches; the permanent boards and agencies and their functions; and the ethos and practises of the two bodies. No major difficulties were envisioned by the Joint Committee in bringing the two churches together, and the committee recommended that the two highest judicatories authorize the preparation of a Plan of Union, to be ready not later than 1968. After extended debate, the recommendation was approved by the Reformed Church synod by a vote of 246 to 16, and unanimously by the Presbyterian assembly.

To assist the Joint Committee in its preparation of the Plan of Union, one hundred consultants—fifty from each denomination— were called together in Louisville in January of 1966, along with representatives of the boards and agencies of the churches. The discussions resulted in the conclusion that many details of structure, and the writing of a new confession of faith, should be left to a provisional council of the new united church, rather than seeking to resolve all matters in the plan of union itself.

At the 1966 session of the General Assembly of the Presbyterian Church in the U.S., it was voted, much to the surprise of many, to become a full participant in the Consultation on Church Union, an effort now encompassing nine major Protestant denominations. There were some in the Reformed Church who wanted to call off any further conversations with the Presbyterian Church, and others who wanted the Reformed Church also to become a full participant in the Consultation. After some fancy parliamentary footwork, the 1966 General Synod voted to instruct the Permanent Committee on Interchurch Relations to study the possibility of Reformed Church participation in the Consultation with instructions to report its findings to the 1967 General Synod. The Synod also voted to ask the Presbyterian Church what its intentions were in regard to the Reformed Church—did the Consultation hold priority, or should the Joint Committee press forward in preparation of the Plan of Union?

A five-man sub-committee of the Interchurch Relations Committee made a thorough study of the Consultation and the *Prin-*

ciples of Church Union, held discussions with the executive committee of the Consultation, and attended working groups of the
Consultation. They came to the following four conclusions:

1. Participation by the Reformed Church in (a) preparation of
a plan of union with the Presbyterian Church, U.S., and (b) The
Consultation on Church Union can be carried on at the same time
with integrity, because the first involves the development of a *plan
of union* for immediate consideration, while the second involves a
consultation having long range, rather than immediate, implications.
2. The Reformed Church in America-Presbyterian Church U.S.
union proposal holds priority, and final action on that plan of
union should be taken before any plan of union coming out of the
Consultation on Church Union is presented for vote by either
church.
3. Participation in the Consultation by both churches would
place them in the same relationship to the Consultation, and would
assist both in their preparation for the Reformed Church in
America-Presbyterian Church U. S. union proposal.
4. The new united church which would result from union of the
Reformed Church in America and the Presbyterian Church U. S.
would have to make its own decision regarding its relationship
to the Consultation.[9]

The Ad Interim Committee on the Consultation on Church Union
of the Presbyterian Church, U. S., and the Interchurch Relations
Committee of that church concurred in these four conclusions,[10]
and the 1967 General Assembly of the Presbyterian Church adopted
these four statements as its response to the query from the Reformed Church as to its intentions. The Interchurch Relations
Committee of the Reformed Church unanimously recommended to
the 1967 General Synod that the Reformed Church become a full
participant in the Consultation, on the basis of its study, the above
conclusions, and the following statement on "The Unity We Seek
to Manifest," adopted by the 1966 General Synod:

" . . . we of the Reformed Church in America resolve to manifest
the God-given unity of the Church by working to overcome our
divisions. The ways and means to unity are not always known. The
goal of unity is a venture of faith. Therefore trusting in the Holy
Spirit for guidance, we shall be open to His counsel, *willing to
converse with any church,* ready to cooperate with all Christians,
committed to participate in councils of churches on all levels, prepared to merge with any church when it is clearly the will of God,

eager to heal the brokenness of the Body of Christ in all ways made known to us, until all are one, so that the world may know that the Father has sent the Son as Savior and Lord."[11]

After extended discussion, the General Synod, by the narrow margin of 148 to 128, defeated the recommendation.

Meanwhile, the Joint Committee of Twenty-Four had been making steady progress in the preparation of the Plan of Union. The first study draft, with a proposed Form of Government for the united church, appeared in January 1967. The new church would be called the Presbyterian Reformed Church in America, and would be governed along traditional presbyterian lines, with a unicameral board called a consistory. The consistory would be composed of elders, fulfilling the functions formerly assigned to elders and deacons. Each presbytery would be able to have a General Pastor, who would function along the lines of a General Presbyter in the United Presbyterian Church.

The second study draft, *Proposals Regarding The Worship and Work of The Church and Its Discipline* (Richmond & New York: Presbyterian Book Stores and the Reformed Church Book Store), and the third study draft, *Proposals on Theology, and on the Witness and Structures of the Church,* appeared later in 1967. The *Directory for the Worship of God* is a worship manual prepared by the Presbyterian Church in the U. S. with the United Presbyterian Church, and is included in the draft for study. The agreement on worship calls for *The Liturgy and Psalms* of the Reformed Church to be the liturgy officially approved for use by the new church, with *The Book of Common Worship* of the Presbyterian Church as an additional resource. The document on the work of the church corresponds to a document in use in the Presbyterian Church, and the discipline is a blend of the similar disciplines of the two churches. The doctrinal standards of the new church would include those of both churches, namely, the Belgic Confession, the Heidelberg Catechism, the Westminster Confession of Faith, and the Westminster Shorter Catechism. In addition, the new church would commit itself to attempt to write a new confession after union occurs. No attempt is made to devise a structure for the united church; rather, a provisional council, composed of equal numbers from both churches, would work out structural schemes after union.

If the Revised Plan of Union is approved by the General Synod and the General Assembly in 1968, and by two-thirds of the Reformed Church classes and three-fourths of the Presbyterian presbyteries, and then ratified by the General Synod and General Assembly in 1969, the consummating General Assembly of the Presbyterian Reformed Church in America could take place in 1970. If the Plan of Union is rejected by either church, one or other of the two less desirable alternatives for the future of the Reformed Church (mentioned above on p. 88) may well come into being. If, on the other hand, the union is accomplished, the Reformed Church in America may at long last overcome her "ecumenical-separatist split personality." She will then be able to witness by her life to a belief that concern for Christian unity has consequences also for church union with denominations similar in background, theology, and tradition. She will then show that her ancient motto, "Eendracht Maakt Macht,"[12] is being taken seriously at home as well as abroad.

Bibliography

(Note: The Archives of the General Synod of the Reformed Church in America are located in the Gardner Sage Library of the Theological Seminary of the Reformed Church in America.)

Acts and Proceedings of the General Synod of the Reformed Church in America, Vol. I-XLVII. New York: Board (later Department) of Publication, Reformed Church in America. 1771-1967.

An Address of the Board of Managers of the United Foreign Missionary Society to the Three Denominations United in This Institution. New York: J. Seymour. 1817.

Annual Report, American Board of Commissioners for Foreign Missions. Boston: Crocker & Brewster; later, T. P. Marvin. 1810-1858.

Annual Report, Board of North American (formerly Domestic) *Missions.* New York: Board (later Department) of Publication, Reformed Church in America. 1832-1962.

Annual Report, Board of World (formerly Foreign) *Missions.* New York: Board (later Department) of Publication, Reformed Church in America. 1832-1962.

Bast, Henry, *An Appeal to the Ministers and Laymen of the Chicago and Iowa Synods.* Grand Rapids: Don Van Ostenberg. 1947.

Board of World Missions, *India in Transition.* New York: Board of World Missions, R. C. A. 1964.

Brennecke, Gerhard, *Weltmission in Oekumenischer Zeit.* Stuttgart: Evang. Missionsverlag. 1961.

Briggs, Charles A., *American Presbyterianism.* Edinburgh: T. & T. Clark. 1885.

Briggs, Charles A., *Church Unity.* New York: Charles Scribner's Sons. 1909.

Brinkerhoff, Joseph, *The History of the True Reformed Dutch Church in the United States of America.* New York: E. B. Tripp. 1873.

Brower, Wm. L., *Organic Union Not Favored.* New York: Wm. L. Brower. 1929.

Brower, Wm. L., *Some Thoughts on the Report of the Fact Finding Committee at the Meeting of the General Synod of Reformed Church in America.* New York: Wm. L. Brower. 1929.

Brown, Willard Dayton, *History of the Reformed Church in America.* New York: Board of Publication, Reformed Church in America. 1928.

Calvin Forum. Grand Rapids: Christian Reformed Church. (Vol. 1-21) 1935-1956.

Centennial Discourses. New York: Board of Publication, Reformed Church in America. 1877.

Centennial of the Theological Seminary of the Reformed Church in America. New York: Board of Publication, Reformed Church in America. 1885.

Chambers, Talbot W., et al, *The Name of the Reformed Dutch Church.* New York: Sanford, Harroun & Co. 1867.

Christian Intelligencer. New York: Reformed Church in America. (Vol. 1-105.) 1829-1934.

Church Herald, The. Grand Rapids: Reformed Church in America. (Vol. 1-18) 1944-1962.

Conference on Union between the Reformed Church in America and the Reformed Church in the United States. Philadelphia: Reformed Church Publication House. 1888.

Corwin, Edward Tanjore, *A Digest of Constitutional and Synodical Legislation of the Reformed Church in America.* New York: Board of Publication, Reformed Church in America. 1906.

Corwin, Edward Tanjore, *History of the Reformed Church, Dutch.* New York: The Christian Literature Co. 1895.

Corwin, Edward Tanjore, *Manual of the Reformed Church in America* (2d, 3d, 4th, and 5th Editions). New York: Board of Publication, Reformed Church in America. 1869, 1879, 1902, 1922.

Corwin, Edward Tanjore, *Manual of the Reformed Protestant Dutch Church.* New York: Board of Publication, Reformed Church in America. 1859.

Curti, Merle, *The Growth of American Thought.* New York: Harper and Brothers Publishers. 1943.

Demarest, William Henry Steele, *History of Rutgers College, 1776-1924.* New Brunswick, New Jersey: Rutgers College. 1924.

Digest of Facts. Joint Committee on Union. 1947.

Dubbs, Joseph Henry, *Historic Manual of the Reformed Church in the United States.* Lancaster: Inquirer Printing Co. 1885.

Ehrenstrom, Nils, et al, *Institutionalism and Church Unity.* New York: Association Press. 1963.

Fagg, John Gerardus, *Forty Years in South China.* New York: Board of Publication, Reformed Church in America. 1894.

Gaustad, Edwin Scott, *Historical Atlas of Religion in America.* New York: Harper & Row, Publishers. 1962.

Gloede, Guenther, *Oekumenische Profile.* Stuttgart: Evang. Missionsverlag GmbH. 1961.

Good, James I., *History of the Reformed Church in the United States 1725-1792.* Reading: Daniel Miller, Publisher. 1899.

Gregg, William, *History of the Presbyterian Church in Canada.* Toronto: Presbyterian Printing and Publishing Co. 1885.

Gunn, Alexander, *Memoirs of the Rev. John H. Livingston.* New York: Rutgers Press. 1829.

Hageman, Howard G., *Lily Among the Thorns.* New York: The Half Moon Press. 1953.

Hageman, Howard G., *Pulpit and Table.* Richmond: John Knox Press. 1962.

Handy, Robert T., *We Witness Together.* New York: Friendship Press. 1956.

Hansen, Maurice G., *The Reformed Church in the Netherlands.* New York: Board of Publication, Reformed Church in America. 1884.

Harmelink, Herman III, *The Decline of the Reformed Church in Manhattan.* New Brunswick, N. J.: Unpublished thesis. 1958.

Hastings, Hugh (ed.), *Ecclesiastical Records, State of New York.* (7 vol.) Albany: J. B. Lyon (and State of New York). 1901-1916.

Hermelink, Jan, *Kirchen in der Welt.* Stuttgart: Verlagsgemeinschaft Burckhardthaus-und Kreuz-Verlag GmbH. 1959.

Hinkamp, Jonathan James, *Into the Land of Canaan.* Unpublished Manuscript. 1961.

Hogg, William Richey, *Ecumenical Foundations.* New York: Harper & Brothers. 1952.

Iglehart, Charles W., *A Century of Protestant Christianity in Japan.* Rutland, Vt.: Charles E. Tuttle Co. 1959.

Intelligencer-Leader, The. Holland, Michigan (later Grand Rapids): Reformed Church in America. 1934-1943.

International Review of Missions (Vol. I-LI). London: Oxford University Press. 1912-1962.

James, Bartlett B., *The Labadist Colony in Maryland.* Baltimore: The Johns Hopkins Press. 1899.

Klein, H. M. J., *The History of the Eastern Synod of the Reformed Church in the United States.* Lancaster: The Eastern Synod. 1943.

Latourette, Kenneth Scott, *A History of Christianity.* New York: Harper & Brothers. 1953.

Leader, The. Holland, Michigan: Hope College. 1906-1934.

Leiby, Andrew C., *The Revolutionary War in the Hackensack Valley.* New Brunswick: Rutgers University Press. 1962.

Livingston, John H., *The Everlasting Gospel.* New York: 1804.

Mackay, James Hutton, *Religious Thought in Holland During the Nineteenth Century.* London: Hodder and Stoughton. 1911.

Magazine of the Reformed Dutch Church (Vol. 1-5). New Brunswick: Rutgers Press. 1826-1829.

Maury, P. et al, *History's Lessons for Tomorrow's Mission.* Geneva: World's Student Christian Federation. 1960.

Maxson, Charles Hartshorn, *The Great Awakening in the Middle Colonies.* Chicago: University of Chicago Press. 1920.

McCoy, Charles Sherwood, *The Covenant Theology of Johannes Cocceius.* New Haven: Yale University. 1956. (unpublished thesis)

McNeill, John T., *Modern Christian Movements.* Philadelphia: The Westminster Press. 1954.

McNeill, John T., *Unitive Protestantism.* New York: Abingdon Press. 1930.

Mercersburg (Quarterly) Review, The. Chambersburg: M. Kieffer. (Vol. 1-25) 1848-1878.

Messler, Abraham, *Eight Memorial Sermons.* New York: A. Lloyd. 1873.

Minutes of the Coetus and Conferentie (1738-1767). New York: Board of Publication, Reformed Church in America. 1859.

Mol, Johannis J., *Churches and Immigrants.* The Hague: Albani. 1961.

Mol, Johannis J., *Theology and Americanization: The effects of Pietism and Orthodoxy on Adjustment to a New Culture.* New York: Columbia University. 1960. (unpublished thesis)

Nederlands Archief voor Kerkgeschiedenis. 's-Gravenhage: Martinus Nijhoff. 1962. (Vol. XIV)

Neill, Stephen C. and Ruth Rouse, *A History of the Ecumenical Movement.* Philadelphia: The Westminster Press. 1954.

Nijenhuis, Willem, *Calvinus Oecumenicus.* 's-Gravenhage: Martinus Nijhoff. 1958.

Nichols, James Hastings, *History of Christianity 1650-1950.* New York: The Ronald Press Co. 1956.

Nichols, James Hastings, *Romanticism in American Theology.* Chicago: The University of Chicago Press. 1961.

Nixon, Leroy, *Reformed Standards of Unity.* Grand Rapids: Society for Reformed Publications. 1952.

Pieters, Albertus, et al, *Classis Holland Minutes 1848-1858.* Grand Rapids: Grand Rapids Printing Co. 1943.

Plan of Union 1949. Joint Committee on Union. 1949.

Protestant Quarterly Review, The (Vol. 1-11). Philadelphia: W. S. Young. 1844-1854.

Raven, John Howard, *Biographical Record, Theological Seminary, New Brunswick, New Jersey.* New Brunswick: The Seminary. 1934.

Reformed Church Monthly, The. (Vol. I-IX) Philadelphia: Loag. 1868-1876.

Reformed Church Review, The. (Vol. 1-25 Series 4, Vol. 1-5 Series 5) Philadelphia: Reformed Church Publication Board. 1897-1926.

Reformed Quarterly Review, The. (Vol. 26-43) Philadelphia: Reformed Church Publication Board. 1879-1896.

Ritschl, Albrecht, *Geschichte des Pietismus in der Reformirten Kirche.* Bonn: Adolph Marcus. 1880.

Rodgers, John, *A Charge to Rev. Mr. Joseph Bullen.* New York: 1799.

Romig, Edgar F., *Tercentenary of the Reformed Church in America.* New York: Board of Publication, Reformed Church in America. 1928.

Scholten, Sharon T., *The Rise and Decline of the Reformed Church in Oklahoma.* New Brunswick, N. J.: Unpublished thesis. 1957.

Shafer, Luman J., *The Christian Alternative to World Chaos.* New York: Round Table Press. 1940.

Shafer, Luman J., *The Christian Mission in Our Day.* New York: Friendship Press. 1944.

Smith, H. Shelton, et al, *American Christianity* (Vol. 1 & 2). New York: Charles Scribner's Sons. 1960-1963.

The Address and Constitution of the New York Missionary Society. New York: T. & J. Swords. 1796.

True Reformed Dutch Church, *Acts and Proceedings of the General Synod.* New York: D. Fanshaw. 1824.

Trinterud, Leonard J., *The Forming of an American Tradition.* Philadelphia: The Westminster Press. 1949.

Vanderlaan, E. C., *Protestant Modernism in Holland.* London: Oxford University Press. 1924.

Van Eyck, Wm. O., *Landmarks of the Reformed Fathers.* Grand Rapids: The Reformed Press. 1922.

Van Zandt, A. B., *The Rightful Name of the Protestant Reformed Dutch Church.* New York: Sanford, Harroun & Co. 1867.

Veenschoten, William, *Should the Reformed Church in America Continue a Separate Organization?* Albany: Burdick & Taylor. 1884.

Wagenaar, J., *"Reveil" en de "Afscheiding."* Heerenveen: J. Hepkema. 1880.

Walker, Williston, *A History of the Christian Church.* (Rev. ed.) New York: Charles Scribner's Sons. 1959.

Warnshuis, A. Livingston, *The Church in South Fukien.* London: Oxford University Press. 1939.

Winterhager, Juergen W., *Kirchen-Unionen des Zwanzigsten Jahrhunderts.* Zurich: Gotthelf Verlag. 1961.

Notes

Chapter I. Introduction

1. Nijenhuis, Willem, *Calvinus Oecumenicus* ('s-Gravenhage: Martinus Nijhoff, 1958). Calvin is also described as a leading ecumenical figure in a recent German book by Guenther Gloede, *Oekumenische Profile* (Stuttgart: Evang. Missionsverlag GmbH., 1961). Many of the other profiles in this book are of leaders in the Reformed tradition.

2. Reformed Church in America, *Centennial Discourses* (New York: Board of Publication of the Reformed Church in America, 1877), p. 377.

3. Nixon, Leroy, *Reformed Standards of Unity* (Grand Rapids: Society for Reformed Publications, 1952), p. 8.

4. Corwin, Edward Tanjore, *Manual of the Reformed Church in America* (fourth edition; New York: Board of Publication of the Reformed Church in America, 1902), p. 11. The English presence may have resulted from sympathy for the Dutch in their anti-Spanish, anti-Catholic struggle.

5. The geographical distinctions "Eastern" and "Western" are not absolute. There were, of course, some more liberal Westerners and conservative Easterners. They refer to the majority view of the members of the church east or west of the Alleghenies.

Chapter II. The Struggle for Ecclesiastical Independence (1628-1771)

1. Corwin, Edward Tanjore, *Manual of the Reformed Church in America* (fourth edition; New York: Board of Publication of the Reformed Church in America, 1902), pp. 32-3.
2. *Ibid.*, p. 26.
3. *Ibid.*, p. 33.
4. *Ibid.*
5. *Ibid.*, pp. 57-9.
6. *Ibid.*, p. 87. Also Van Cleef, Paul D., in *Centennial Discourses of the Reformed (Dutch) Church in America* (New York: Board of Publication of the Reformed Church in America, 1877), p. 357.
7. Corwin, *op. cit.*, pp. 29-30.
8. Dubbs, Joseph Henry, *Historic Manual of the Reformed Church in the United States* (Lancaster, Pa.: Inquirer, 1885), pp. 209-10.
9. Muzelius, Frederick, *Minutes, General Synod*, Vol. I, 1747, p. xiii.
10. Good, James I., *History of the Reformed Church in the United States 1725-1792* (Reading: Daniel Miller, 1897), p. 130.
11. Dubbs, *op. cit.*, p. 174; also Corwin, *op. cit.*, p. 105.
12. Good, *op. cit.*, pp. 474-7.
13. *Ibid.*, p. 479.
14. *Ibid.*, p. 480.
15. *Ibid.*, p. 484.
16. Mol, Johannis J., *Theology and Americanization: The Effects of Pietism and Orthodoxy on Adjustment to a New Culture* (unpublished thesis, Columbia University, New York, 1960). Dr. Mol describes this phenomenon at length in his thesis.
17. *Minutes*, General Synod, Vol. I, pp. xciv-xcvii.

18. *Ibid.*, p. cxxxi. Also Corwin, *op. cit.*, pp. 107-110.
19. Demarest, W. H. S., *A History of Rutgers College 1766-1924* (New Brunswick: Rutgers College, 1924), p. 65.
20. *Ibid.*, p. 66.
21. *Ibid.*, p. 67.
22. *Ibid.*, pp. 38-9.
23. Corwin, *op. cit.*, pp. 114-6.
24. Demarest, *op. cit.*, pp. 57-8.
25. *Ibid.*, pp. 79-80.
26. *Minutes*, General Synod, Vol. I, pp. cxxvii-cxxviii.
27. *Ibid.*, p. 2.
28. *Ibid.*, p. 9.

Chapter III. The Struggle for Ethnic-Cultural Survival (1771-1820)

1. *Minutes*, General Synod, 1773, p. 39.
2. *Ibid.*, October 1780, p. 84.
3. Reformed Church in America, *Centennial Discourses* (New York: Board of Publication of the Reformed Church in America, 1877), p. 130.
4. Leiby, Andrew C., *The Revolutionary War in the Hackensack Valley* (New Brunswick: Rutgers University Press, 1962).
5. *Minutes*, General Synod, October 1784, pp. 124-5.
6. Demarest, W. H. S., *A History of Rutgers College 1766-1924* (New Brunswick: Rutgers College, 1924), pp. 173-4.
7. *Ibid.*, p. 177.
8. *Ibid.*, pp. 179-80. (Also *Minutes*, General Synod, 1794, pp. 261-3).
9. *Ibid.*, p. 203.
10. *Minutes*, General Synod, 1804, p. 334.
11. *Ibid.*, p. 339.
12. *Ibid.*, 1817, pp. 33-4.
13. *Ibid.*, October 1815, p. 9.
14. *Ibid.*, 1784, p. 108.
15. *Ibid.*, 1785, p. 132. Similar arrangements were made by the Presbyterian and Congregational churches in the famous "Plan of Union" of 1801.

16. *Ibid.*, 1800, p. 281.
17. *Ibid.*, 1816, pp. 14-6.
18. *Ibid.*, 1821, p. 42. Associate Reformed Minutes for 1821 indicate they were annoyed with the Dutch Reformed for starting a new church near one of theirs.
19. Good, James I., *History of the Reformed Church in the United States 1725-1792* (Reading: Daniel Miller, 1899), p. 50.
20. *Minutes*, General Synod, 1794, p. 258.
21. *Ibid.*, 1800, p. 280.
22. *Ibid.*, 1820, p. 52.
23. *Ibid.*, 1782, p. 99.
24. *Ibid.*, 1785, p. 141.
25. *Ibid.*, 1812, p. 413.
26. *Ibid.*, 1793, pp. 245-6.
27. *Ibid.*, 1788, p. 181.
28. *Ibid.*, 1789, pp. 191-3. Corwin's *Manual* (p. 543) calls him "Jennings," so "Ginnings" is no doubt a misspelling.
29. *Ibid.*, 1791, p. 217.
30. *Ibid.*, 1794, p. 264.
31. Corwin, Edward Tanjore, *Manual of the Reformed Church in America* (fourth edition; New York: Board of Publication of the Reformed Church in America, 1902), p. 218. See also Gregg, William, *History of the Presbyterian Church in Canada* (Toronto: Presbyterian Church in Canada, 1885).
32. *The Address and Constitution of the New York Missionary Society* (New York: T. & J. Swords, 1796), p. 13.
33. *Ibid.*, p. 16.
34. *Ibid.*, p. 7.
35. Rodgers, John, *A Charge to Rev. Mr. Joseph Bullen* (New York, 1799). Includes a *Plan for Social Prayer*, pp. 98-9.
36. *The Address and Constitution of the New York Missionary Society*, p. 10.
37. Reformed Church in America, *Tercentenary Studies* (New York: General Synod of the Reformed

Church in America, 1928), p. 493.

38. *Minutes,* General Synod, 1816, pp. 14-6.
39. *An Address of the Board of Managers of the United Foreign Missionary Society to the Three Denominations United in This Institution* (New York: J. Seymour, 1817), p. 4.
40. *Ibid.*
41. *Reformed Review* (Holland, Michigan: Western Theological Seminary, Vol. 17, No. 3, March 1964), p. 15.
42. Corwin, *op. cit.*, p. 240.
43. Livingston, John H., *The Everlasting Gospel* (New York: 1804).
44. *Tercentenary Studies,* p. 493.

Chapter IV. Joint Action in Missions, Federations, and Alliances (1820-1885)

1. Reformed Church in America, *Tercentenary Studies* (New York: General Synod of the Reformed Church in America, 1928), p. 494.
2. *Minutes,* General Synod, 1826, p. 61.
3. *Ibid.,* 1832, p. 89.
4. *Ibid.,* 1833, p. 232.
5. *Ibid.,* 1836, pp. 525-8.
6. *Ibid.,* 1845, p. 494.
7. *Ibid.,* 1855, p. 605.
8. *Ibid.,* 1857, p. 234.
9. *Ibid.,* p. 235.
10. Fagg, John G., *Forty Years in South China* (New York: Board of Publication of the Reformed Church in America, 1894), pp. 184-5.
11. *Ibid.,* p. 188.
12. *Minutes,* General Synod, 1863, p. 337.
13. Fagg, *op. cit.,* p. 196.
14. *Ibid.,* pp. 199-203.
15. *Minutes,* General Synod, 1863, p. 340.
16. Fagg, *op. cit.,* pp. 220-1. Also *Minutes,* General Synod, 1864, p. 490.

17. Fagg, *op. cit.,* p. 223.
18. *Tercentenary Studies,* p. 501.
19. *Minutes,* General Synod, 1867, p. 277.
20. *Ibid.*
21. *Ibid.,* 1874, p. 143.
22. *Ibid.,* 1875, p. 257.
23. Iglehart, Charles W., *A Century of Protestant Christianity in Japan* (Rutland, Vt.: Charles E. Tuttle Co., 1959), pp. 31-2.
24. *Ibid.,* p. 43.
25. *Minutes,* General Synod, 1874, p. 143.
26. Corwin, Edward Tanjore, *A Digest of Constitutional and Synodical Legislation of the Reformed Church in America* (New York: Board of Publication of the Reformed Church in America, 1906), p. 355.
27. *Minutes,* General Synod, 1829, p. 182.
28. *Ibid.,* 1834, pp. 270-3.
29. *Ibid.,* 1846, pp. 65-6.
30. *Ibid.,* 1873, p. 674.
31. Schaf and Nevin, for example. See Nichols, James Hastings, *Romanticism in American Theology* (Chicago: University of Chicago Press, 1961), pp. 164-5.
32. *Minutes,* General Synod, 1849, pp. 455-9.
33. *Ibid.,* 1865, p. 574.
34. *Ibid.,* p. 576.
35. *Ibid.*
36. *Ibid.,* 1868, p. 420.
37. *Ibid.,* 1870, pp. 52-3. The Minutes say "National Council of *Ecclesiastical* Churches," but obviously they mean 'Evangelical.'
38. *Ibid.,* 1873, pp. 673-4. Dr. B. M. Schmucker of Gettysburg was the son of Dr. S. S. Schmucker, who issued an appeal for Protestant church union in 1838.
39. *Ibid.,* 1875, pp. 260-4.
40. True Reformed Dutch Church, *Acts and Proceedings of the General Synod* (New York: D. Fanshaw, 1824), pp. 32-9.
41. Brinkerhoff, Jacob, *The History*

of the True Reformed Dutch Church in the United States of America (New York: E. B. Tripp, 1873), pp. 29-31.

42. Van Eyck, Wm. O., Landmarks of the Reformed Fathers (Grand Rapids: The Reformed Press, 1922), p. 196.

43. Minutes, General Synod, 1848 (September), p. 425.

44. Corwin, Edward Tanjore, Manual of the Reformed Church in America (fourth edition; New York: Board of Publication of the Reformed Church in America, 1902), p. 139.

45. Pieters, Albertus et al, Classis Holland Minutes 1848-1858 (Grand Rapids: Grand Rapids Printing Co., 1943), pp. 122-33.

46. Ibid., p. 206.

47. Ibid., p. 242.

48. Ibid., p. 245.

49. Minutes, General Synod, 1868, p. 461.

50. Ibid., 1870, pp. 96-7.

51. Ibid., 1880, p. 534.

52. Ibid., pp. 535-6.

53. Ibid., 1881, pp. 733-4.

54. Ibid., 1882, p. 68

55. Ibid., 1834, p. 329.

56. Ibid., 1842, pp. 72-3.

57. Ibid., 1843, p. 180.

58. Nichols, op. cit., pp. 60-1.

59. Minutes, General Synod, 1845, pp. 424-30.

60. Ibid., 1846, pp. 30-1; also Nichols, op. cit., p. 224.

61. Ibid., 1847, pp. 137-40.

62. Ibid., 1850, p. 35.

63. Nichols, op. cit., p. 296.

64. Ibid., p. 192.

65. Minutes, General Synod, 1853, p. 317.

66. Ibid., p. 319.

67. Ibid., 1855, p. 535.

68. Corwin, A Digest of Constitutional and Synodical Legislation of the Reformed Church in America, p. 586.

69. Nichols, op. cit., p. 308.

70. Minutes, General Synod, 1870, pp. 51-2.

71. Ibid., 1874, pp. 52-57.

72. Ibid., 1875, pp. 255-9.

73. Ibid., 1876, p. 451; 1877, pp. 723-4.

74. Ibid., 1879, p. 279.

75. Ibid., 1884, p. 459.

76. Ibid., 1843, pp. 184-6.

77. Ibid., 1824, pp. 27-8.

Chapter V. Advance and Retreat (1886-1893)

1. Acts and Proceedings of the General Synod of the Reformed Church in America, 1886, p. 126.

2. Ibid., pp. 126-7.

3. Ibid., p. 127.

4. Ibid., 1887, p. 368.

5. Ibid., p. 369.

6. Ibid., pp. 363-4.

7. Ibid., p. 365.

8. Conference on Union Between the Reformed Church in America and the Reformed Church in the United States (Philadelphia: Reformed Church Publishing House, 1888), pp. iii, iv.

9. Minutes, General Synod, 1888, p. 617.

10. Conference on Union Between R. C. A. and R. C. U. S. (note 8).

11. Ibid., p. iv.

12. Ibid., pp. 6-13.

13. Ibid., pp. 13-14, 17.

14. Ibid., pp. 18-34.

15. Ibid., pp. 40-41, 35, 43.

16. Ibid., pp. 43-52.

17. Ibid., pp. 52-62.

18. Ibid., pp. 72-85.

19. Ibid., pp. 85-94.

20. Ibid., pp. 103-114.

21. Ibid., pp. 114-124.

22. Ibid., pp. 126-7.

23. Ibid., p. iv.

24. Minutes, General Synod, 1888, p. 607.

25. Ibid.

26. Ibid., pp. 618-9.

27. Ibid., 1889, pp. 843-5.

28. Ibid., 1890, p. 128.

29. *Ibid.*, p. 129.
30. *Ibid.*, 1891, pp. 352-4.
31. *Ibid.*, pp. 354-6.
32. *Ibid.*, p. 358, 357.
33. *The Christian Intelligencer* (New York), Vol. 63, January 13, 1892, p. 4.
34. *Ibid.*, March 2, 1892, p. 4.
35. *Ibid.*, March 2, 1892, p. 14.
36. *Ibid.*, March 16, 1892, p. 14.
37. *Ibid.*, January 13, 1892, pp. 4-5.
38. *Ibid.*, February 3, 1892, p. 3.
39. *Ibid.*, March 9, 1892, p. 14.
40. *Ibid.*, March 30, 1892, p. 14.
41. *Ibid.*, March 2, 1892, p. 1.
42. *Ibid.*
43. *Ibid.*, February 24, 1892, p. 3.
44. *Ibid.*, April 27, 1892, p. 1.
45. *Minutes*, General Synod, 1892, pp. 577-584.
46. *The Christian Intelligencer*, June 15, 1892, p. 1.
47. *Ibid.*, September 14, 1892, pp. 1-2.
48. *Ibid.*, September 14, 1892, pp. 1-2; October 12, 1892, p. 1.
49. *Ibid.*, February 1, 1893, p. 94.
50. *Ibid.*, February 8, 1893, p. 111.
51. *Ibid.*, March 15, 1893, p. 214.
52. *Ibid.*, March 22, 1893, p. 224.
53. *Ibid.*, March 1, 1893, p. 165; March 15, 1893, p. 214; March 22, 1893, p. 224; March 29, 1893, pp. 243, 251, 254; April 5, 1893, p. 264.
54. *Ibid.*, April 5, 1893, p. 264.
55. *Ibid.*, March 29, 1893, p. 251.
56. *Ibid.*, April 5, 1893, p. 262.
57. *Ibid.*, March 29, 1893, p. 243.
58. *Minutes*, General Synod, 1893, p. 817.
59. *Ibid.*, p. 818.

Chapter VI. *New Efforts to Federate and Unite (1893-1930)*

1. *Minutes*, General Synod, 1891, pp. 343-5.
2. *Ibid.*, 1893, pp. 821-3.
3. *Ibid.*, 1894, p. 140.
4. *Ibid.*, pp. 139-40.
5. *Ibid.*, 1902, pp. 127-8.
6. *Ibid.*, 1905, pp. 152-4.

7. *Ibid.*, 1904, pp. 747-8.
8. *Ibid.*, 1906, pp. 507-9.
9. *Ibid.*, 1911, p. 171.
10. *Ibid.*, 1914, p. 142.
11. *Ibid.*, 1919, pp. 813-7.
12. *Ibid.*, 1927, pp. 445-6.
13. Smith, H. Shelton et al, *American Christianity*, Vol. II (New York: Chas. Scribner's Sons, 1963), pp. 363, 394.
14. *Minutes*, General Synod, 1904, p. 747.
15. *Ibid.*, 1906, p. 499. Delegates included a relative, Dr. H. Harmeling.
16. *Ibid.*, 1919, p. 930.
17. *Ibid.*, 1920, p. 207.
18. *Ibid.*, p. 209.
19. *The Christian Intelligencer*, Vol. 65, March 28, 1894, p. 238.
20. *Ibid.*, p. 325.
21. *Minutes*, General Synod, 1902, pp. 122-5; 1903, p. 395.
22. *Ibid.*, 1903, p. 401.
23. *Ibid.*, 1904, p. 748.
24. *Ibid.*, 1914, pp. 138-9.
25. *Ibid.*, 1917, pp. 145-6.
26. *Ibid.*, 1927, pp. 447-8.
27. Scholten, Sharon T., *The Rise and Decline of the Reformed Church in Oklahoma* (New Brunswick, N. J.; Unpublished thesis, 1957), p. 15.
28. *Ibid.*, p. 35, quoting *The Christian Intelligencer*, March 1, 1911.
29. Personal conversation with W. H. S. Demarest, 1956. This statement is evidence of a) the provincial attitude of some Dutch Reformed leadership; and b) recognition of the Reformed Church's failure to have a *distinctive* role to play in America.
30. *Minutes*, General Synod, 1918, p. 478.
31. *Ibid.*, p. 479.
32. *Ibid.*, 1919, p. 816.
33. *Ibid.*, p. 815.
34. *Ibid.*, 1920, pp. 144-8.
35. *Ibid.*, p. 149.
36. *Ibid.*, p. 151.

37. *The Christian Intelligencer,* Vol. 92, May 18, 1921, p. 308.
38. *Minutes,* General Synod, 1921, p. 514.
39. *Ibid.,* 1928, p. 784.
40. *Ibid.,* p. 785.
41. *Ibid.,* 1929, pp. 144-7.
42. *Ibid.,* pp. 188-9. The committee undoubtedly knew that the conservatives would raise the issues of "Lutheranism," and "Arminianism," hence came out ahead of time against the German Reformed and for the Presbyterians.
43. *Ibid.,* pp. 194-6.
44. *The Christian Intelligencer,* Vol. 100, June 19, 1929, p. 387.
45. *Ibid.*
46. Brower, Wm. L., *Some Thoughts on the Report of the Fact Finding Committee at the Meeting of the General Synod of R. C. A.* (New York: William L. Brower, 1929).
47. *Ibid.,* pp. 1-2.
48. *Ibid.,* p. 2.
49. *Ibid.*
50. *Ibid.,* pp. 2-3.
51. Brower, Wm. L., *Organic Union Not Favored* (New York: William L. Brower, 1929), p. 2.
52. *Ibid.,* p. 3.
53. *Ibid.,* p. 3.
54. *Ibid.,* p. 9.
55. *Ibid.,* pp. 11-13.
56. *Ibid.,* p. 17.
57. Scholten, Walter A., in *The Christian Intelligencer,* Vol. 100, November 6, 1929, p. 710.
58. Brinckerhoff, Theodore, in *The Christian Intelligencer,* Vol. 101, April 30, 1930, p. 285; May 7, 1930, p. 302; May 14, 1930, p. 317; May 21, 1930, p. 335; May 28, 1930, p. 348; June 4, 1930, p. 362.
59. VanEss, Jacob, in *The Christian Intelligencer,* Vol. 101, February 26, 1930, p. 134.
60. Kuizenga, J. E., in *The Leader,* February 2, 1930, p. 8.
61. *The Christian Intelligencer,* May 14, 1930, p. 316.

62. *Ibid.*
63. *Minutes,* General Synod, 1930, p. 580.
64. *Ibid.,* p. 585.
65. *Ibid.,* pp. 585-6.
66. Demarest, W. H. S., *Speech Nominating E. S. Worcester at General Synod,* 1923. (Manuscript in R. C. A. Archives.)
67. Worcester, E. S., *Memoranda on the Standards,* 1923. (Manuscript in R. C. A. Archives.)
68. *Ibid.*
69. Printed document circulated by G. H. Hospers, et al. (Copy in R. C. A. Archives.)
70. Letter from Peter Moerdyke to Henry Lockwood (In R. C. A. Archives.), June 2, 1923.
71. *New Brunswick Daily Home News,* June 13, 1923.
72. *Ibid.,* June 14, 1923.
73. Letter from G. H. Hospers to W. H. S. Demarest (in R. C. A. Archives.), June 26, 1923.
74. Letter from G. H. Hospers to J. H. Raven (in R. C. A. Archives.), July 17, 1923.
75. *Minutes,* General Synod, 1886, pp. 95-100.
76. *Ibid.,* 1901, pp. 1099, 1121.
77. *Ibid.,* 1902, pp. 99-100.
78. *Ibid.,* 1908, Report of Board of Foreign Missions, pp. x-xi.
79. *India in Transition* (New York: Board of World Missions, R. C. A., 1964), pp. 4-5.
80. *Minutes,* General Synod, 1919, Report of Board of Foreign Missions, p. xvii. Also *Ibid.,* 1920, p. xi.
81. Ironically, the western section strongly supports the overseas mission budget of the church in spite of its *united* character. Since the depression of the 1930's, it has provided the bulk of that budget.

*Chapter VII. Cross-Currents
(1930-1960)*

1. "Stated supply" is a technical term denoting a preacher who is not the installed minister.
2. Burggraaff, Winfield, in *The Christian Intelligencer,* Vol. 101, February 12, 1930, p. 9.
3. *Ibid.*
4. *Minutes,* General Synod, 1930, pp. 556-7.
5. *Ibid.,* 1931, p. 946.
6. *Ibid.,* pp. 949-953.
7. *Ibid.,* 1934, pp. 700-701.
8. *Ibid.,* p. 702.
9. Bast, Henry, *An Appeal to the Ministers and Laymen of the Chicago and Iowa Synods* (Grand Rapids: Don Van Ostenberg, 1947).
10. *Ibid.,* p. 13.
11. *Ibid.,* pp. 5-6
12. *Ibid.,* p. 11.
13. *Minutes,* General Synod, 1947, pp. 121, 123, 124.
14. *Ibid.,* p. 123.
15. *Ibid.*
16. Pieters, Albertus, personal letter to J. W. Ter Louw, December 18, 1947 (Archives of General Synod).
17. Pieters, Albertus, personal letter to J. W. Ter Louw, February 14, 1948 (Archives of General Synod).
18. Luben, Barnerd, personal letter to J. W. Beardslee, Jr., January 30, 1948 (Archives of General Synod).
19. *Ibid.*
20. *Open Letter to Congregations of the Reformed Church in America* (unpublished), April 1948 (Archives of General Synod).
21. Sizoo, Joseph, personal letter to J. R. Mulder, May 4, 1948 (Archives of General Synod).
22. *Minutes,* General Synod, 1948, pp. 173-4.
23. *Ibid.,* 1958, p. 135; 1959, pp. 122-3; 1960, p. 113; 1961, pp. 129-30; 1962, pp. 118-20; 1963, pp. 107-8.
24. *The Christian Intelligencer,* Vol. 112, June 13, 1941, p. 5.
25. Greenway, Leonard, in *The Christian Intelligencer,* July 11, 1941, p. 10.
26. Greenway, Leonard, in *Calvin Forum,* October 1941.
27. Kuiper, R. B., in *Presbyterian Guardian,* October 10, 1941 (reprint in Archives of General Synod).
28. Benes, L. H. Jr., in *Intelligencer Leader,* Vol. 112, November 7, 1941, p. 5.
29. Romig, Edgar F., personal letter to J. W. Beardslee, Jr., October 15, 1941 (Archives of General Synod).
30. Beardslee, J. W., Jr., personal letter to Edgar F. Romig, October 18, 1941 (Archives of General Synod).
31. Quoted in mimeographed report of Committee on Doctrine, Morals, and Usages of the Classis of New York, 1941 (Archives of General Synod).
32. *Ibid.*
33. *Minutes,* General Synod, 1942, p. 518.
34. *The Church Herald,* Vol. V, October 22, 1948, p. 17.
35. *Ibid.,* December 3, 1948, p. 9.
36. Sizoo, Joseph, personal letter to J. R. Mulder, May 4, 1948 (Archives of General Synod).
37. *Minutes,* General Synod, 1949, pp. 71-74.
38. *Ibid.,* 1937, pp. 146-7.
39. *Ibid.,* 1938, p. 455.
40. *Ibid.,* 1945, p. 143.
41. *Ibid.,* pp. 145-51.
42. *Minutes,* First Meeting of Joint Committee (Pittsburgh), September 27-28, 1945 (unpublished).
43. *Minutes,* Second Meeting of Joint Committee (Holland, Mich.), February 26-27, 1946 (unpublished).
44. *Digest of Facts.* Joint Committee on Union, 1947.

45. *The United Presbyterian* (Pittsburgh: June 17, 1946) p. 11.
46. *Minutes,* Meeting of Joint Committee, June 6-7, 1946 (unpublished.
47. *Minutes,* Meeting of Joint Committee, December 1, 1947 (unpublished); also *Plan of Union 1949.* Joint Committee on Union, 1949, p. 8.
48. *The Church Herald,* Vol. IV, January 3, 1947, p. 17.
49. Fikse, Henry, in *The Church Herald,* Vol. IV, March 21, 1947, pp. 8-9, 20.
50. *Ibid.*
51. Kuyper, L. J., in *The Church Herald,* Vol. IV, April 18, 1947, p. 11.
52. Hankamp, G., in *The Church Herald,* Vol. IV, April 18, 1947, p. 10.
53. *Minutes,* General Synod, 1947, p. 156.
54. Classis of Grand Rapids, *Report of Committee on Church Union,* November 15, 1948 (unpublished, Archives of General Synod).
55. *The Church Herald,* Vol. VI, January 28, 1949, pp. 12-13.
56. *Ibid.*
57. Oggel, M. V., *Church Union? Yes, In Christ's Name!* (Manuscript, 1949, Archives of General Synod).
58. *The Church Herald,* Vol. VI, February 18, 1949, p. 18.
59. *Ibid.,* February 25, 1949, p. 8.
60. *Ibid.,* March 25, 1949, p. 8.
61. *Ibid.,* April 22, 1949, p. 6.
62. *Ibid.,* May 6, 1949, pp. 11, 22.

63. *Ibid.*
64. Dykstra, B. D., in *The Church Herald,* Vol. VI, April 1, 1949, p. 8.
65. Jansen, Frederick W., *The Church Herald,* Vol. VI, April 15, 1949, p. 15.
66. *Ibid.,* April 29, 1949, p. 12.
67. *Ibid.*
68. *Plan of Union 1949.* Joint Committee on Union, 1949, p. 120.
69. Jamison, Wallace N., *The United Presbyterian Story* (Pittsburgh: The Geneva Press, 1958), p. 217.
70. Personal conversation with Miss Ruth Ransom, former missions executive.

Chapter VIII. Future Prospects

1. *The Church Herald,* Vol. XVIII, May 12, 1961, p. 16.
2. *Ibid.*
3. *Minutes,* General Synod, 1961, p. 142.
4. *Ibid.,* 1962, pp. 350-1, 354.
5. *Ibid.,* p. 124.
6. *Ibid.,* 1963, p. 204.
7. *Ibid.,* 1964, p. 312.
8. *Ibid.,* p. 321.
9. Harmelink, Herman III, *The Reformed Review,* Vol. 20, June 1967, p. 230; also *Minutes,* General Synod, 1967, pp. 265-6.
10. *Commissioners' Handbook,* Presbyterian Church in the U. S., 1967, pp. 139, 190.
11. *Minutes,* General Synod, 1967, p. 266.
12. "In union there is strength."

Index